EVERYBODY'S
BASIC GUITAR SCALES

USEFUL, READY-TO-PLAY SCALES IN STANDARD NOTATION AND TABLATURE

Philip Groeber
David Hoge
Rey Sanchez

CONTENTS

Production: Frank J. Hackinson

Production Coordinator: Philip Groeber

Cover Design: Terpstra Design, San Francisco

Engraving: Tempo Music Press, Inc.

Printer: Tempo Music Press, Inc.

Visit us on the Web at www.fjhmusic.com

ISBN-13: 978-1-56939-539-4

T H E
F·J·H
MUSIC
COMPANY
I N C.

Frank J. Hackinson

GETTING STARTED

The scale patterns in this book are presented in three ways: standard notation; tablature; and fingerboard diagrams. The root notes of each scale are in blue.

Standard Notation

> Line notes = E G B D F
>
> Space notes = F A C E

Tablature

> six lines = strings
>
> numbers = frets

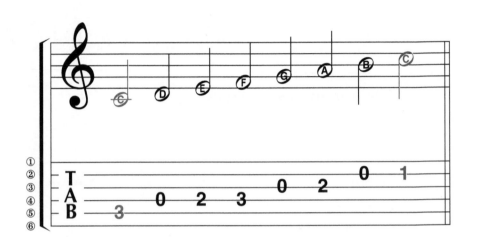

Fingerboard Diagrams

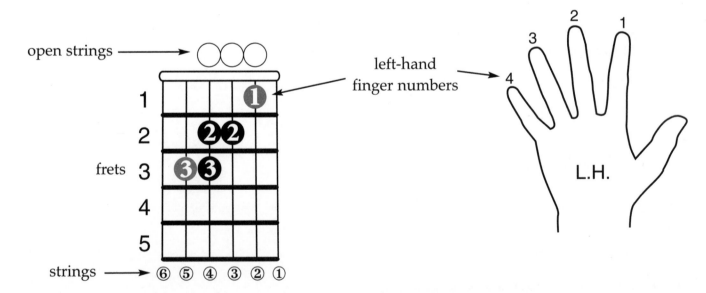

THE IMPORTANCE OF SCALES

The study of scales is crucial to the progress and development of all musicians for the following reasons:

1) Most music is based on some type of scale.

2) Knowledge of scales will help you with composition, song writing, and improvisation.

3) The daily practice of scales helps to improve strength, speed, flexibility, sound, and coordination between the left and right hands.

4) Besides these important facts, scales are just fun to play!

In this book you will learn Major, Minor, and Pentatonic scales in all 12 keys. They are presented in order using the circle of fifths.

PRACTICE TIPS

1. First play the one (or two) octave scale beginning and ending on the root notes (in blue). See the examples indicated on pages 6 and 30. Once you are comfortable with the basic scale, then play *all of the notes* in the range of the box pattern.

2. Memorize the scale pattern, ascending and descending.

3. Begin practicing slowly and evenly, striving for a consistent, legato sound. Use a metronome, starting at ♩ = 60 to ensure a steady beat (pulse). Increase speed gradually.

4. Technique Tips:

- Keep your left hand in a position so that each finger reaches its note with equal effort.

- Right hand—when playing pick style, start with all downstrokes (⊓). Use alternate picking (downstrokes and upstrokes ∨) when the left-hand fingerings are secure. When playing fingerstyle, alternate your fingers (*i-m*, *m-a*, and *i-a*).

- Work on synchronization of the left and right hands in order to produce a clean sound.

5. Finishing Touches:

- Practice scales with your eyes closed to get the "feel" of each pattern.

- Try playing familiar songs by ear using the scale patterns. You may also make up your own music (improvisation).

ABOUT THE BOX PATTERNS

There are five basic fingering patterns that make up all major, minor, and pentatonic scales on the guitar. This is due to the geometric nature of the guitar fingerboard. They are called **box patterns** because the left-hand fingers stay within a basic grid.

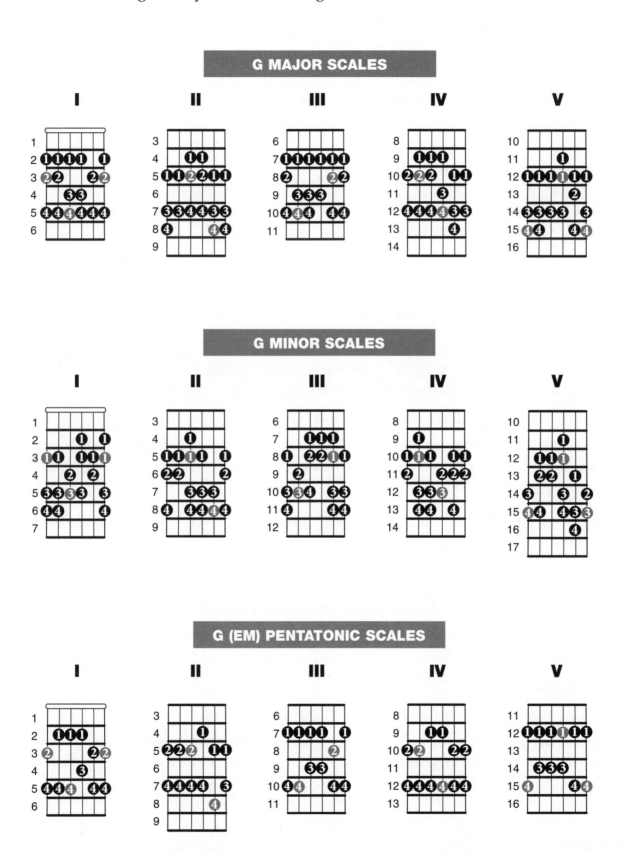

G1032

SCALE THEORY

The Major Scale is the principal scale of Western music. Knowledge of major scales and the concept of **key** is necessary to understand basic harmony. The major scale is constructed according to the following pattern of **whole steps** (notes two frets apart) and **half steps** (notes one fret apart).

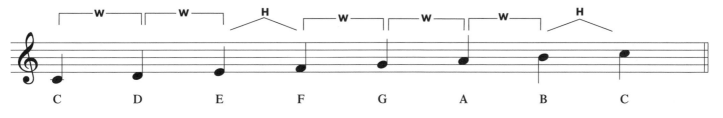

The **Minor Scale** has three forms. This book will focus on the **Harmonic Minor.**

Natural Minor - Identical to the the C major scale but starting on A.

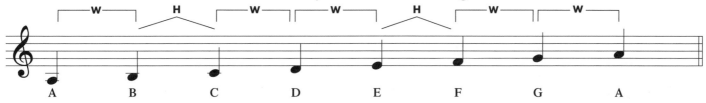

Harmonic Minor - Similar to the natural minor scale but raising the 7th degree by one-half step.

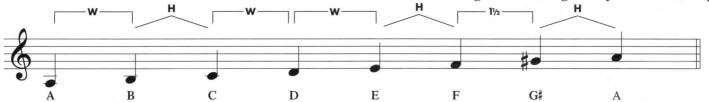

Melodic Minor - Raise the 6th and 7th degrees ascending, but cancel the accidentals descending.

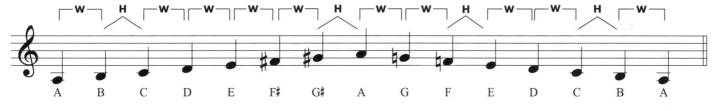

The **Pentatonic Scale** is a five-note scale that is a workhorse in popular music. Both the major and minor pentatonic scales are comprised of the same notes. The only difference is the tonal center (key) that you choose. As seen below, the C pentatonic scale begins and ends on C; the Am pentatonic scale begins and ends on A. The minor pentatonic scale is always the **relative minor** of the major pentatonic scale.

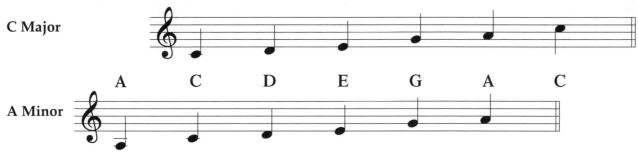

C MAJOR SCALES

1st Position

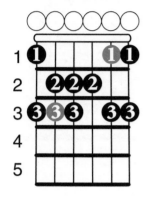

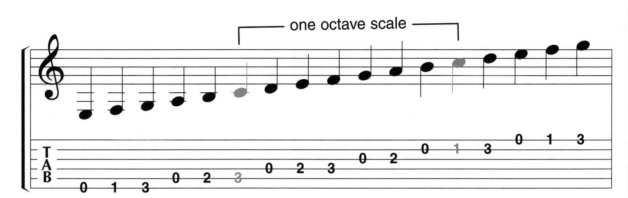

one octave scale

Box Pattern IV
2nd Position

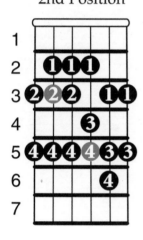

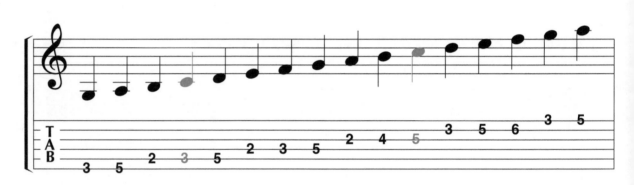

Box Pattern V
5th Position

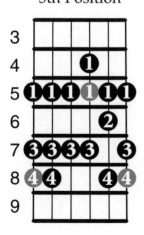

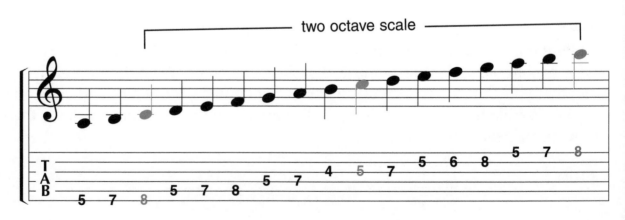

two octave scale

C Major

Box Pattern I
7th Position

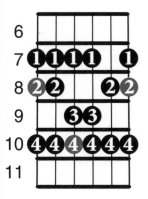

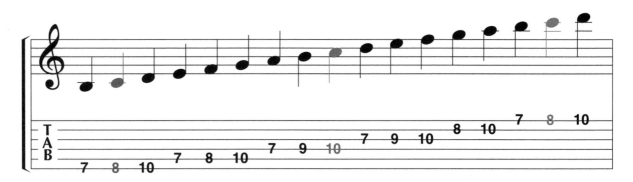

Box Pattern II
10th Position

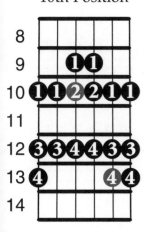

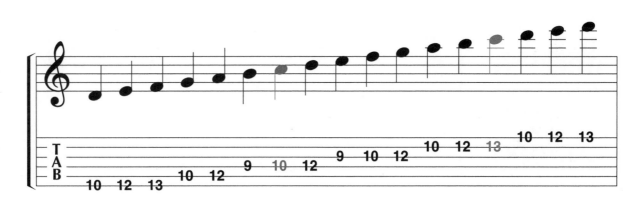

Box Pattern III
12th Position

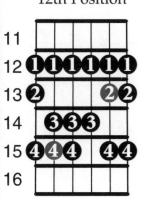

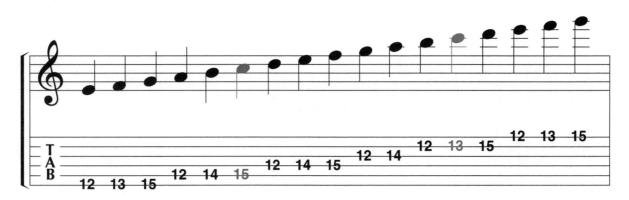

G MAJOR SCALES

First Position

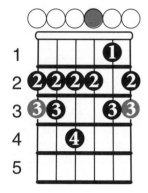

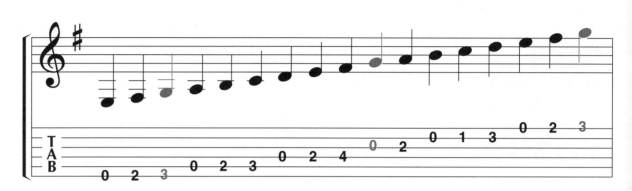

Box Pattern I
2nd Position

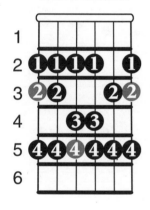

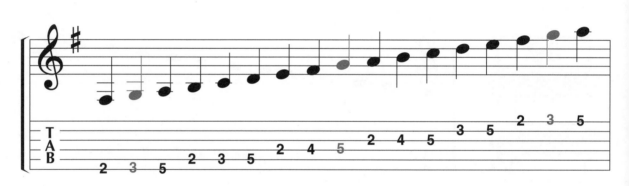

Box Pattern II
5th Position

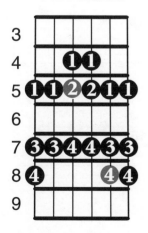

G Major

G A B C D E F# G

Box Pattern III
7th Position

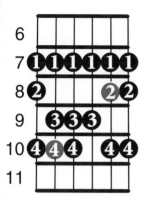

Box Pattern IV
9th Position

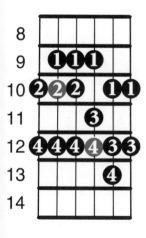

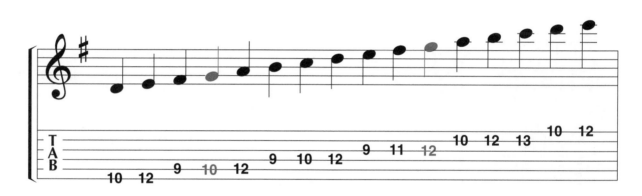

Box Pattern V
12th Position

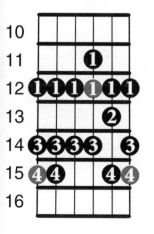

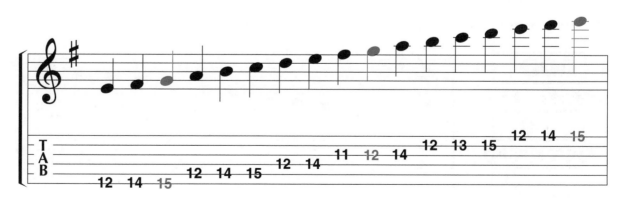

D MAJOR SCALES

2nd Position

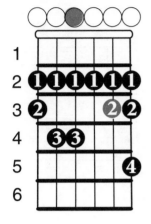

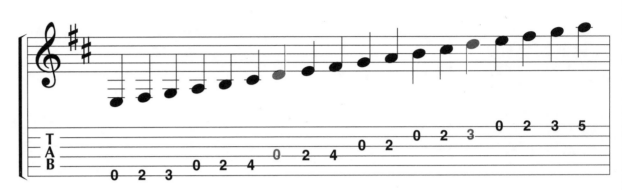

Box Pattern III
2nd Position

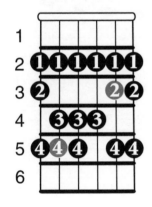

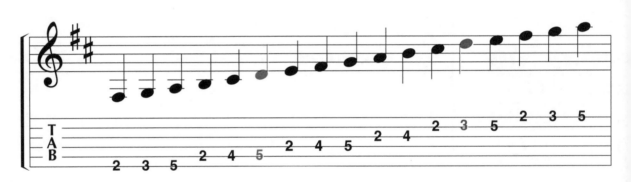

Box Pattern IV
4th Position

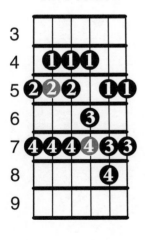

G1032

D Major

Box Pattern V
7th Position

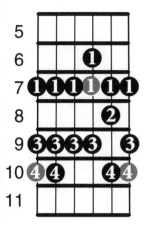

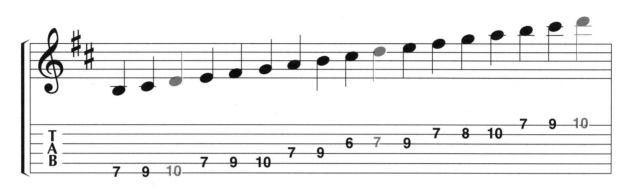

Box Pattern I
9th Position

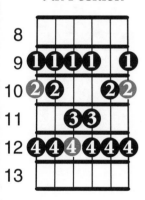

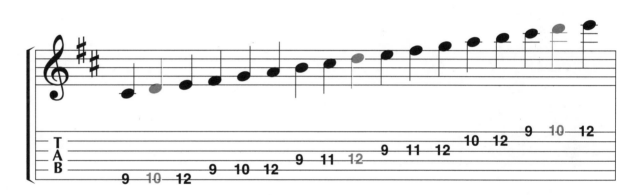

Box Pattern II
12th Position

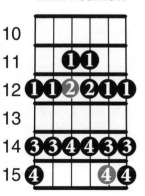

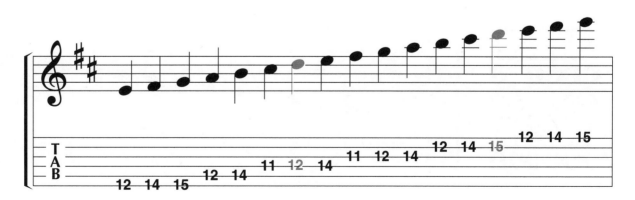

G1032

A MAJOR SCALES

1st Position

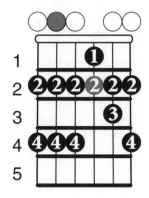

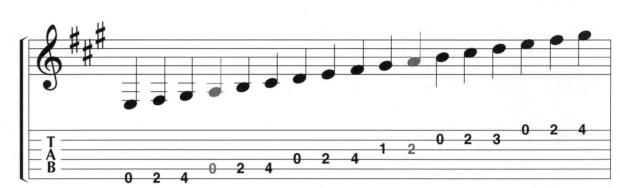

Box Pattern V
2nd Position

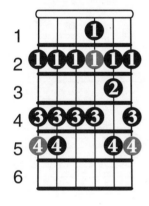

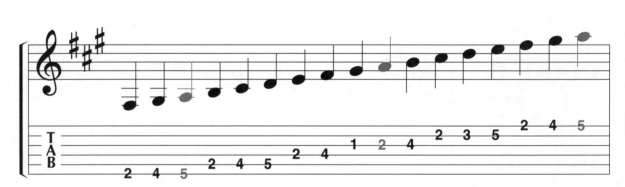

Box Pattern I
4th Position

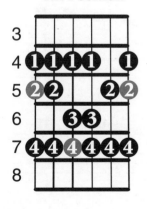

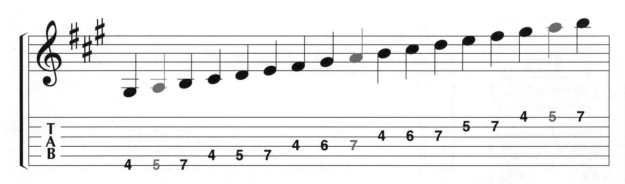

G1032

A Major

A B C# D E F# G# A

Box Pattern II
7th Position

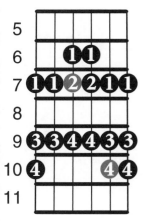

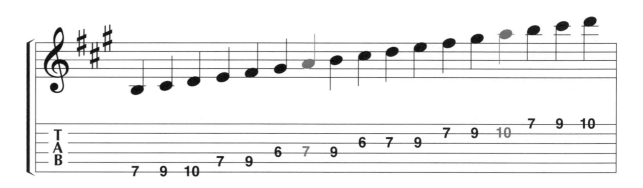

Box Pattern III
9th Position

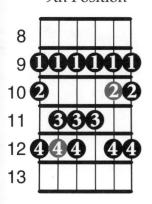

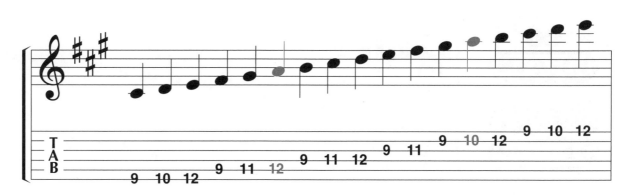

Box Pattern IV
11th Position

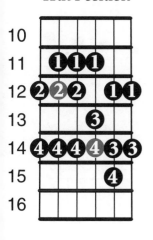

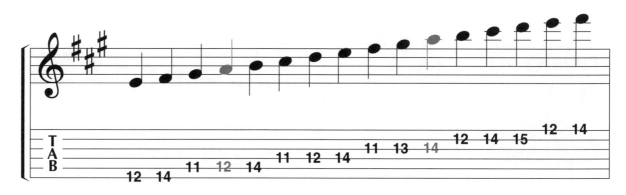

E MAJOR SCALES

1st Position

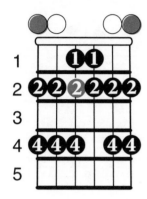

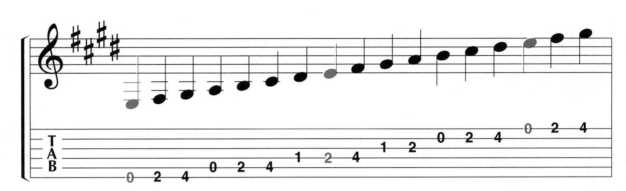

Box Pattern II
2nd Position

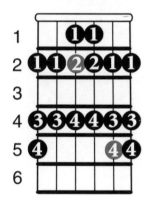

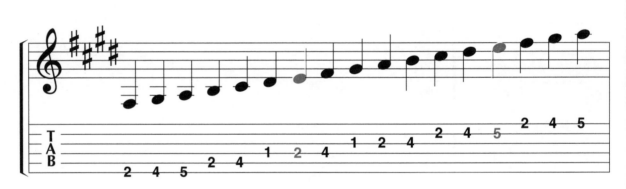

Box Pattern III
4th Position

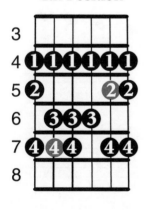

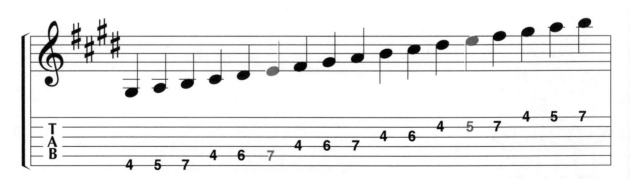

G1032

E Major

Box Pattern IV
6th Position

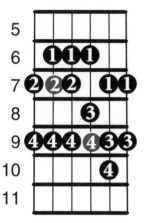

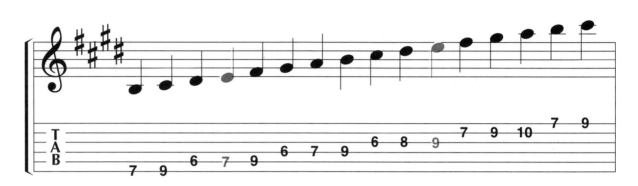

Box Pattern V
9th Position

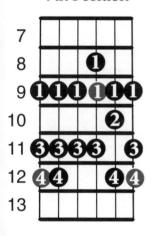

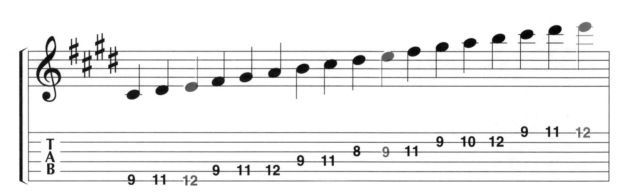

Box Pattern I
11th Position

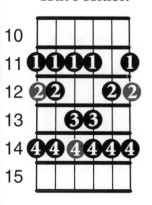

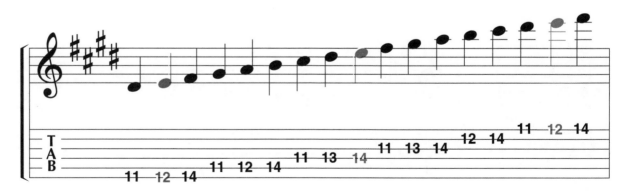

B MAJOR SCALES

1st Position

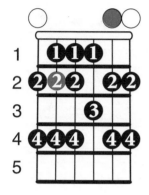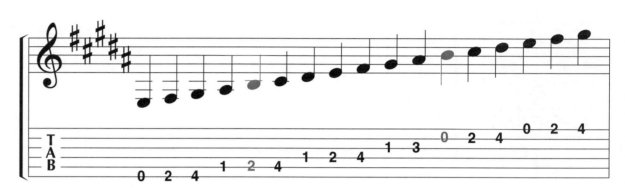

**Box Pattern IV
1st Position**

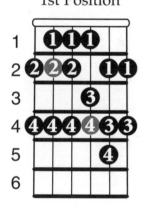

**Box Pattern V
4th Position**

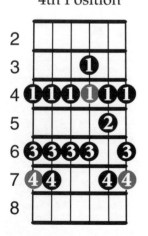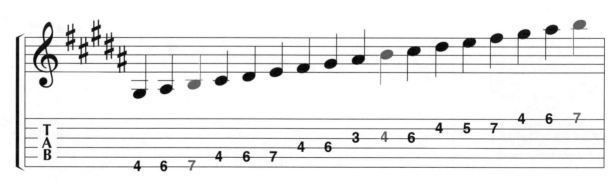

G1032

B Major

B C# D# E F# G# A# B

Box Pattern I
6th Position

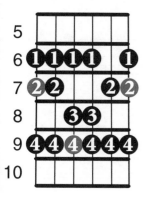

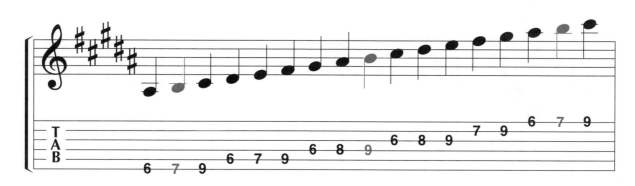

Box Pattern II
9th Position

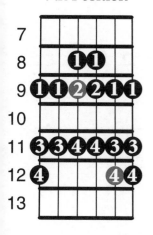

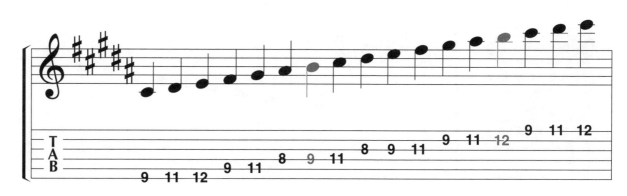

Box Pattern III
11th Position

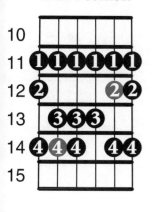

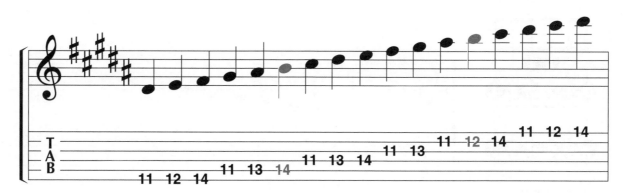

F#/G♭ MAJOR SCALES

1st Position

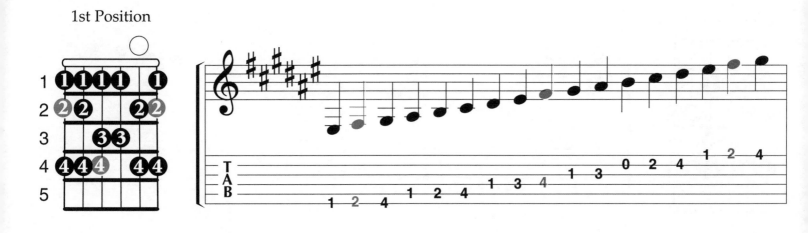

Box Pattern I
1st Position

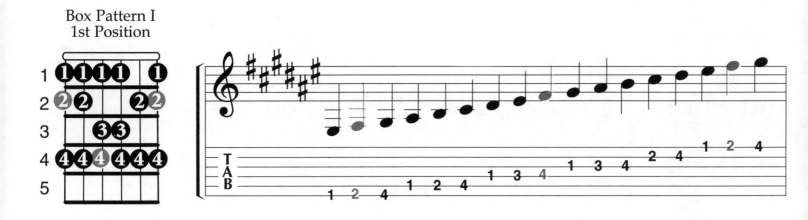

Box Pattern II
4th Position

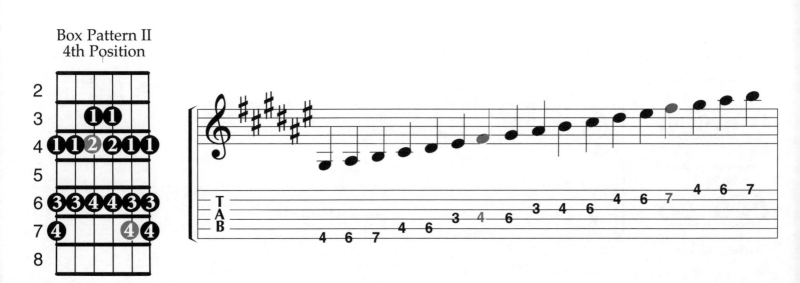

F#/G♭ are **enharmonic notes**. See the **Fact Finder** on page 80.

F# Major

Box Pattern III
6th Position

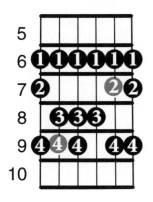
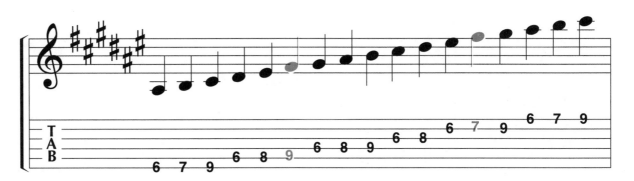

Box Pattern IV
8th Position

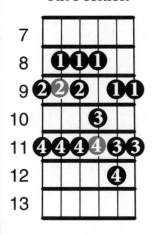
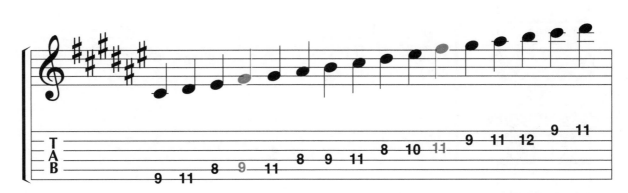

Box Pattern V
11th Position

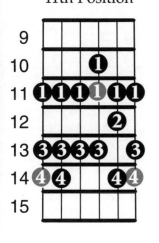
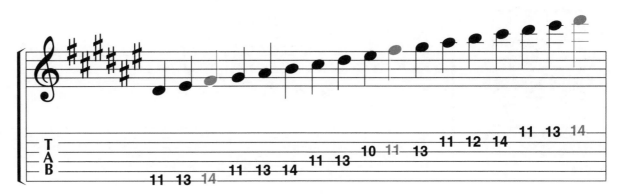

G1032

D♭/C♯ MAJOR SCALES

1st Position

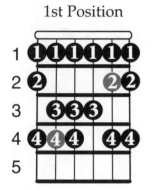

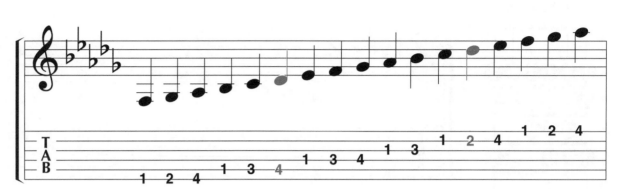

Box Pattern IV
3rd Position

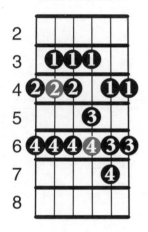

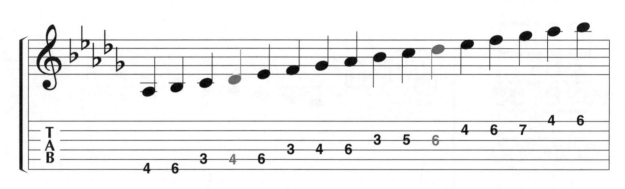

Box Pattern V
6th Position

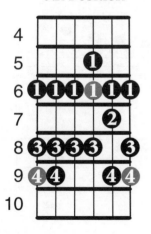

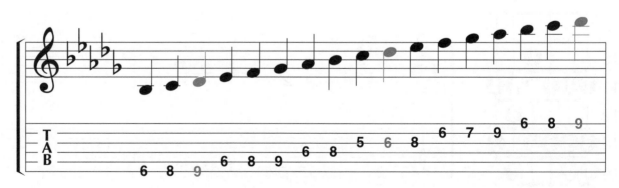

G1032

D♭ Major
D♭ E♭ F G♭ A♭ B♭ C D♭

Box Pattern I
8th Position

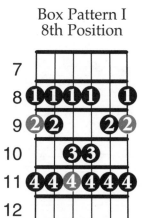

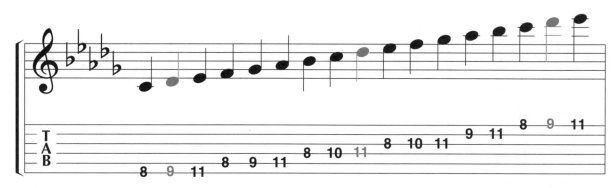

Box Pattern II
11th Position

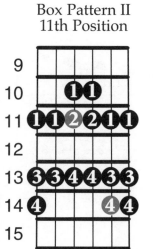

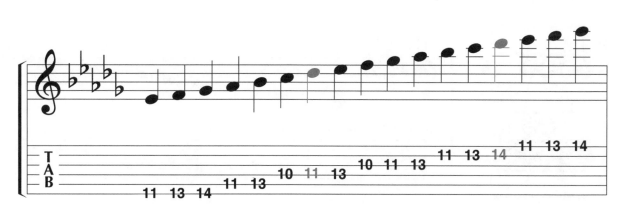

Box Pattern III
13th Position

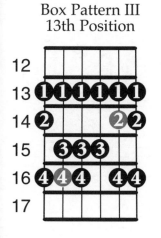

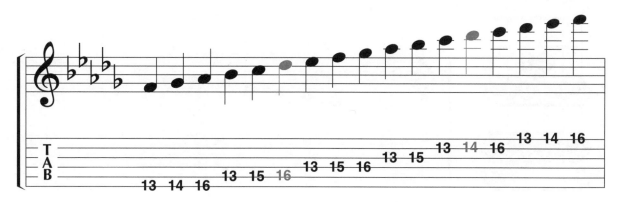

A♭/G♯ MAJOR SCALES

1st Position

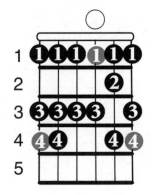

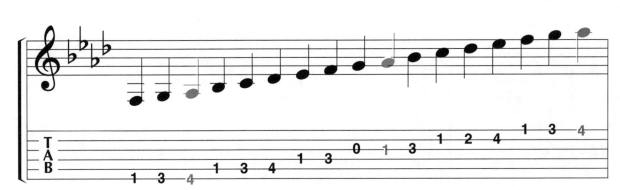

Box Pattern I
3rd Position

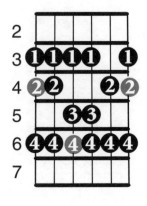

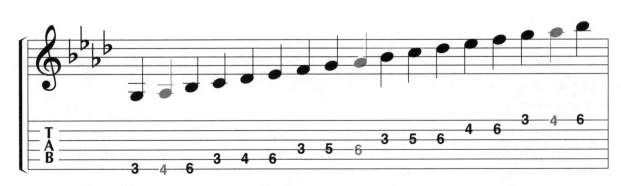

Box Pattern II
6th Position

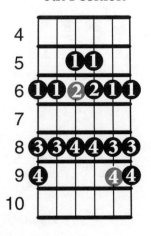

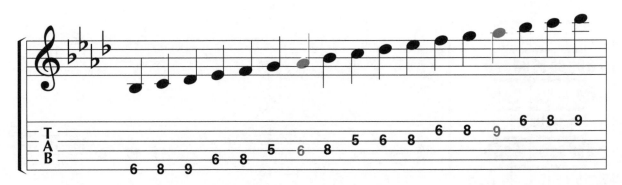

G1032

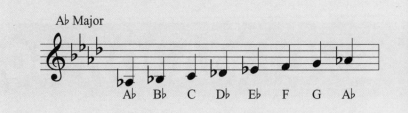

A♭ Major

A♭ B♭ C D♭ E♭ F G A♭

Box Pattern III
8th Position

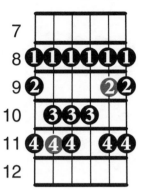

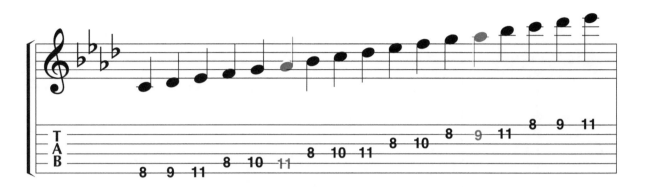

Box Pattern IV
10th Position

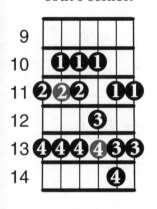

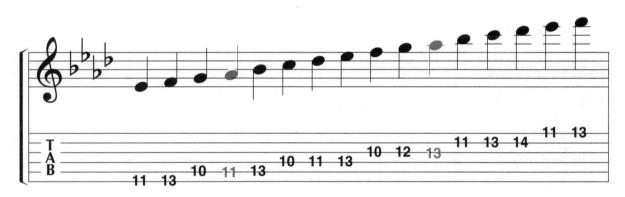

Box Pattern V
13th Position

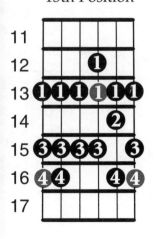

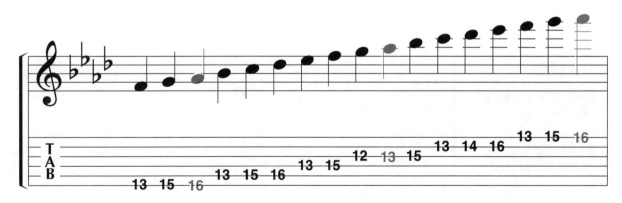

E♭/D♯ MAJOR SCALES

1st Position

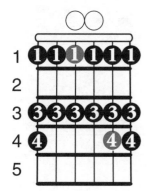
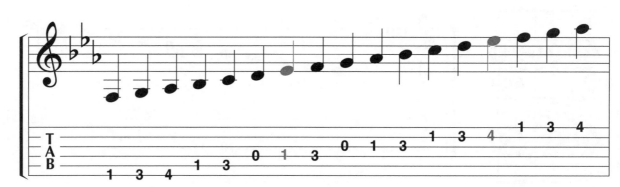

Box Pattern III
3rd Position

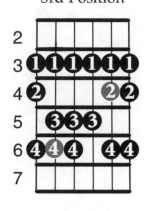

Box Pattern IV
5th Position

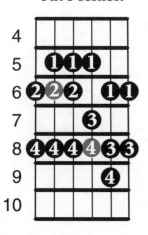
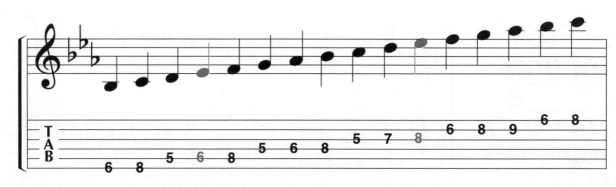

E♭ Major

E♭ F G A♭ B♭ C D E♭

Box Pattern V
8th Position

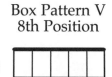
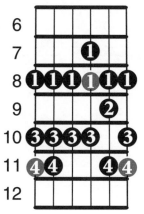

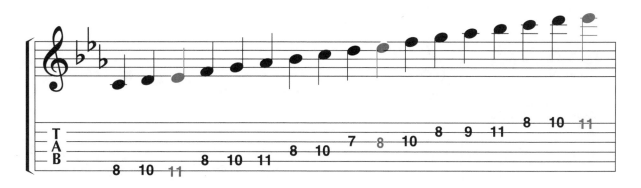

Box Pattern I
10th Position

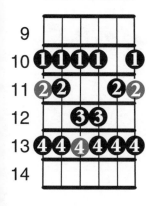

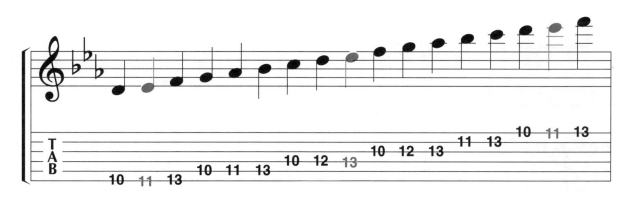

Box Pattern II
13th Position

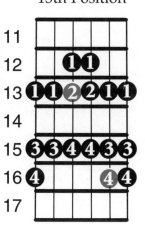

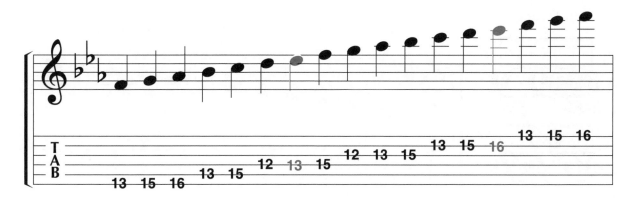

B♭/A♯ MAJOR SCALES

1st Position

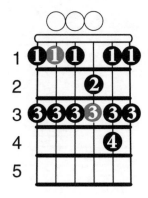

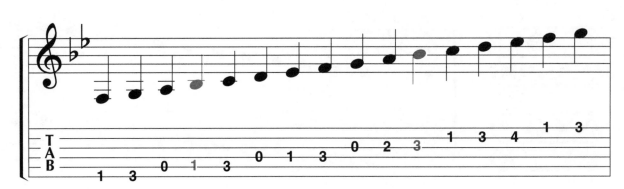

Box Pattern V
3rd Position

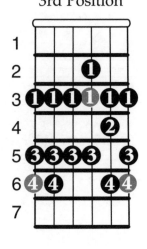

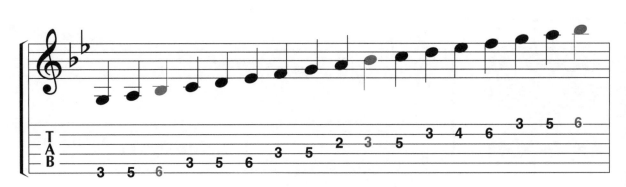

Box Pattern I
5th Position

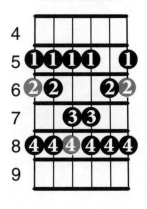

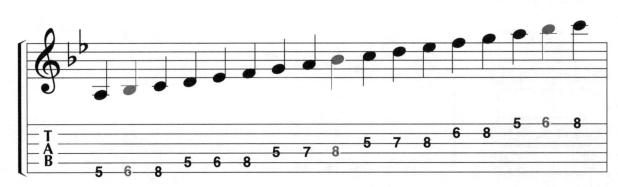

G1032

B♭ Major

B♭ C D E♭ F G A B♭

Box Pattern II
8th Position

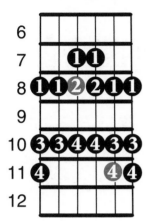

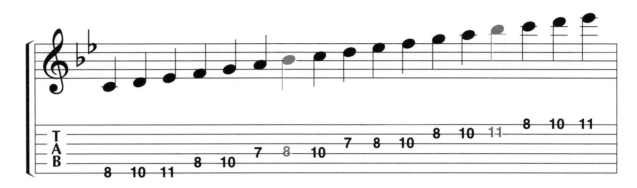

Box Pattern III
10th Position

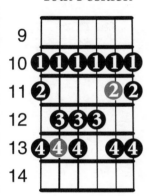

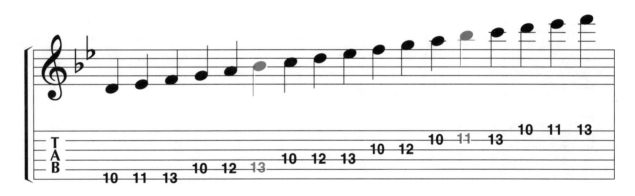

Box Pattern IV
12th Position

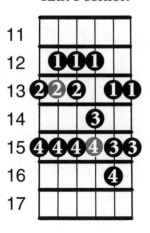

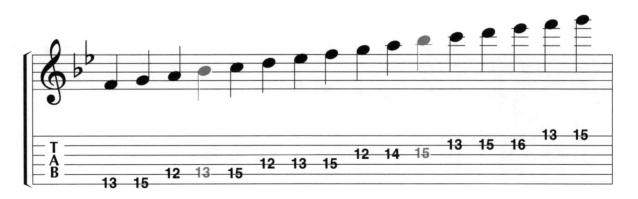

F MAJOR SCALES

1st Position

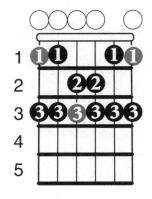

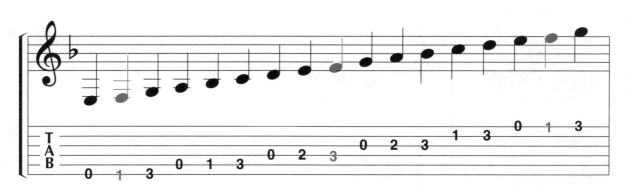

Box Pattern II
3rd Position

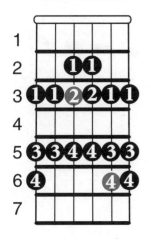

Box Pattern III
5th Position

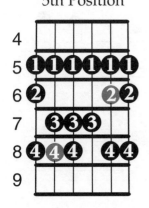

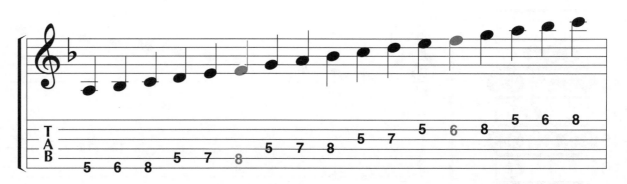

G1032

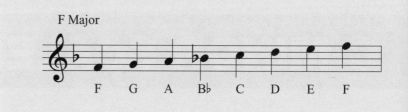

F Major

F G A B♭ C D E F

Box Pattern IV
7th Position

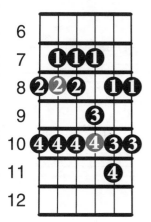

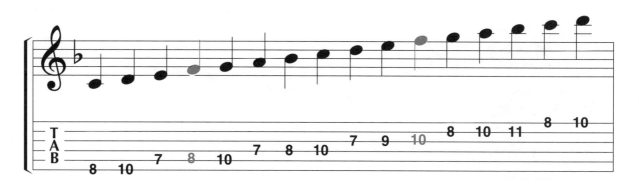

Box Pattern V
10th Position

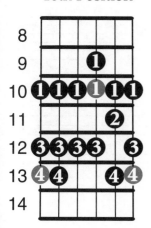

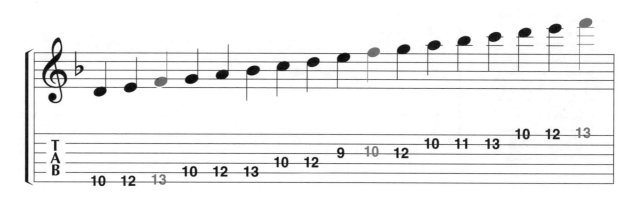

Box Pattern I
12th Position

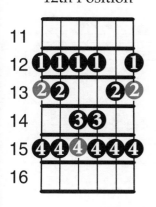

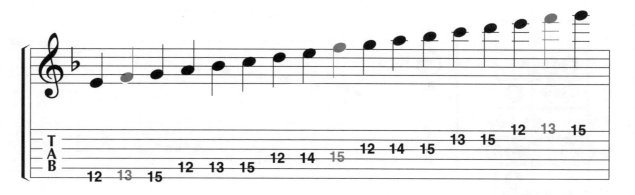

C MINOR SCALES

1st Position

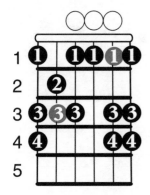

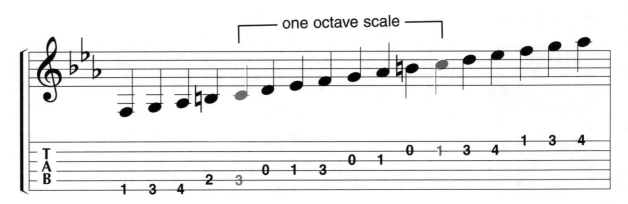

one octave scale

Box Pattern IV
3rd Position

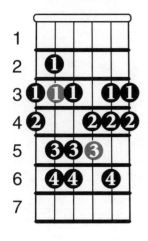

Box Pattern V
5th Position

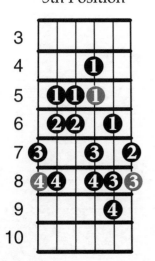

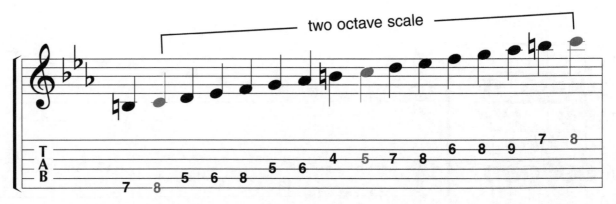

two octave scale

G1032

C Harmonic Minor

C D E♭ F G A♭ B♮ C

Box Pattern I
8th Position

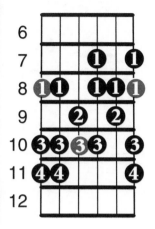

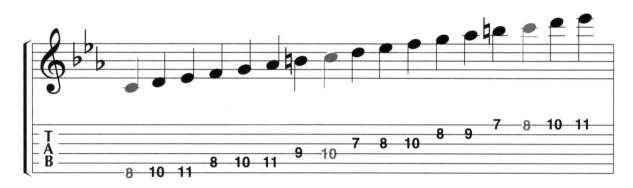

Box Pattern II
10th Position

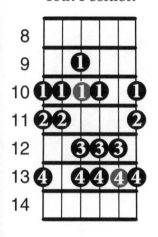

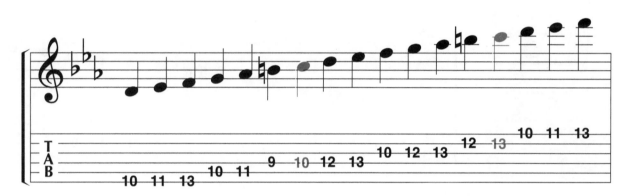

Box Pattern III
13th Position

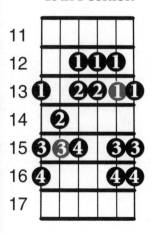

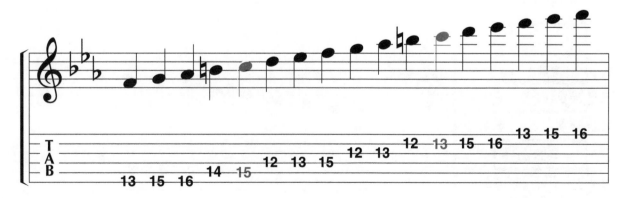

G MINOR SCALES

1st Position

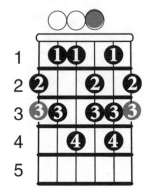

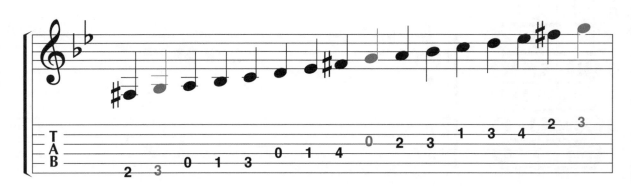

Box Pattern I
3rd Position

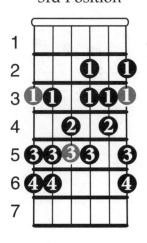

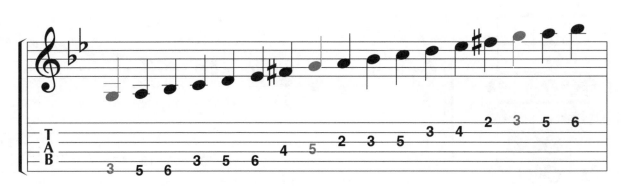

Box Pattern II
5th Position

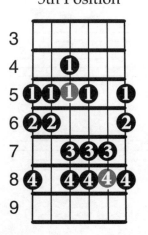

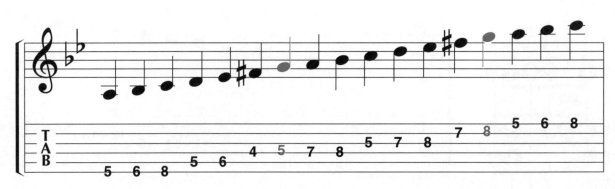

G1032

G Harmonic Minor

G A B♭ C D E♭ F♯ G

Box Pattern III
8th Position

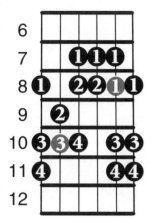

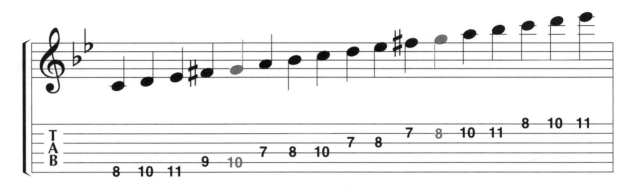

Box Pattern IV
10th Position

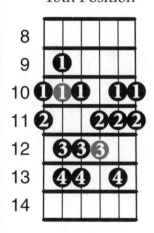

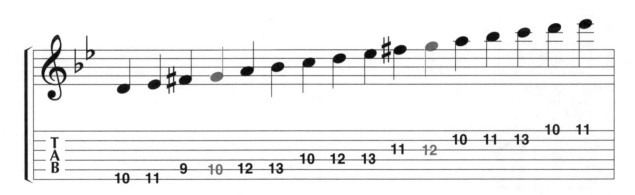

Box Pattern V
12th Position

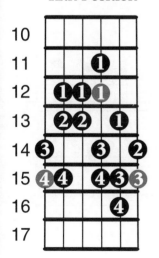

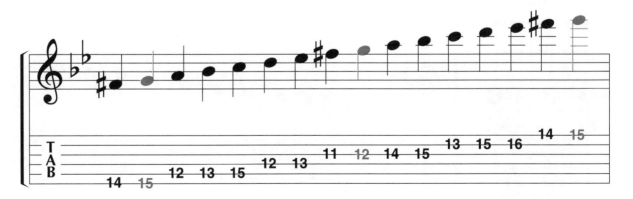

D MINOR SCALES

1st Position

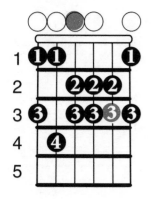

Box Pattern III
3rd Position

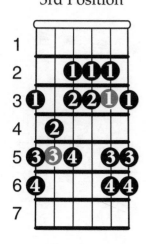

Box Pattern IV
5th Position

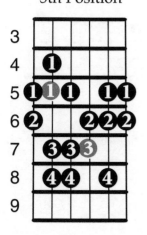

D Harmonic Minor

D E F G A B♭ C# D

Box Pattern V
7th Position

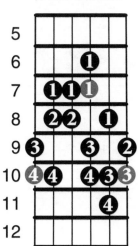

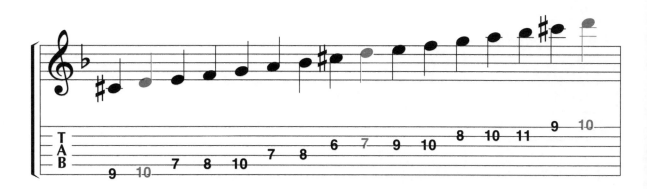

Box Pattern I
10th Position

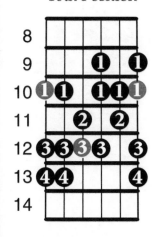

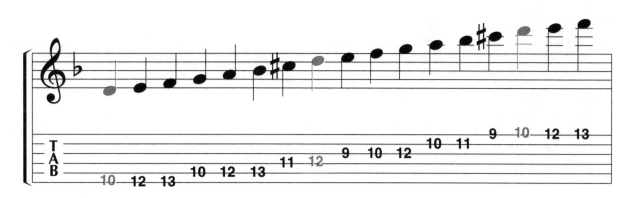

Box Pattern II
12th Position

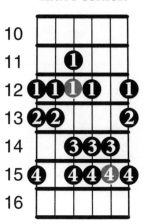

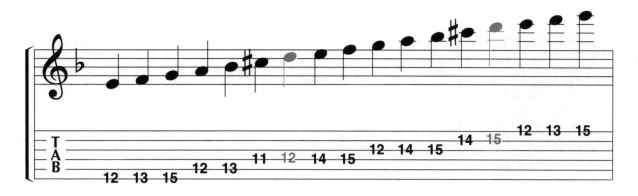

A MINOR SCALES

1st Position

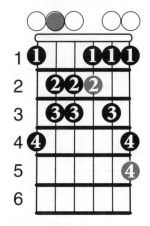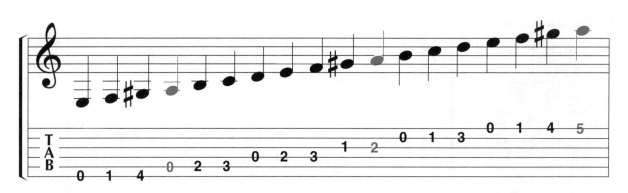

Box Pattern V
2nd Position

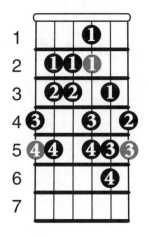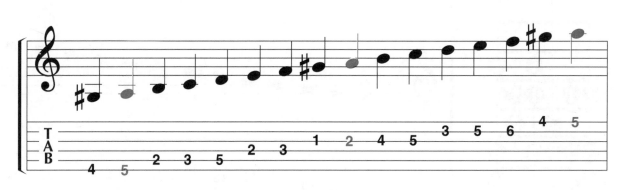

Box Pattern I
5th Position

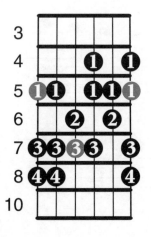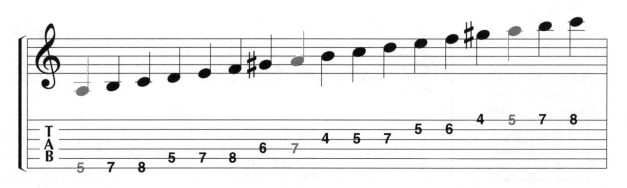

A Harmonic Minor

A B C D E F G# A

Box Pattern II
7th Position

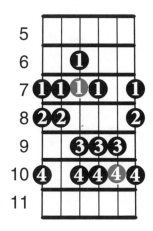

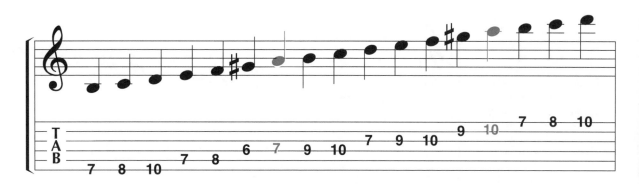

Box Pattern III
10th Position

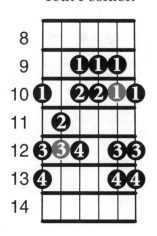

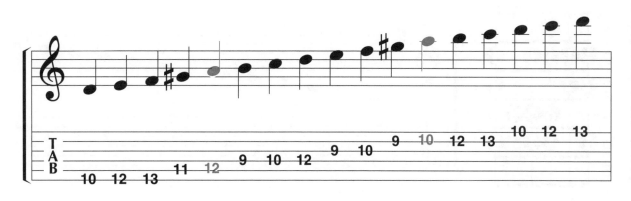

Box Pattern IV
12th Position

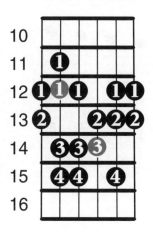

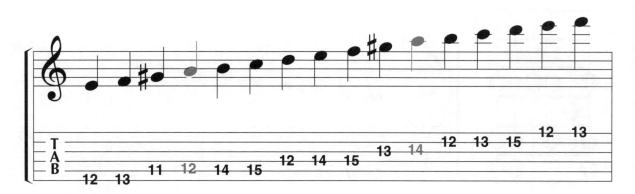

E MINOR SCALES

1st Position

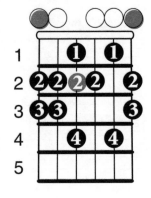

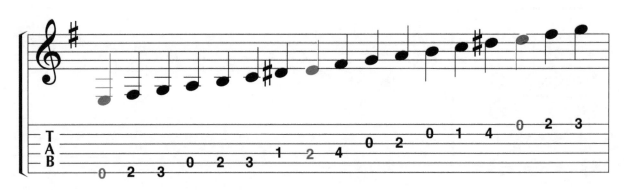

Box Pattern II
2nd Position

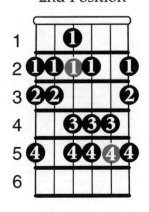

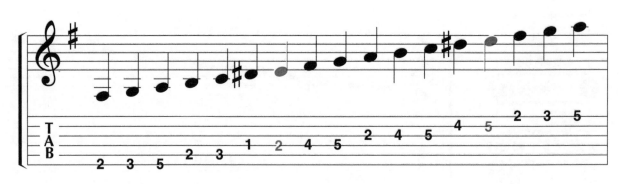

Box Pattern III
5th Position

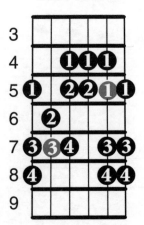

E Harmonic Minor

E F# G A B C D# E

Box Pattern IV
7th Position

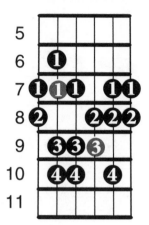

Box Pattern V
9th Position

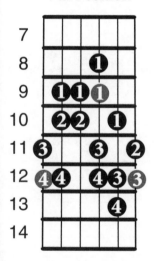

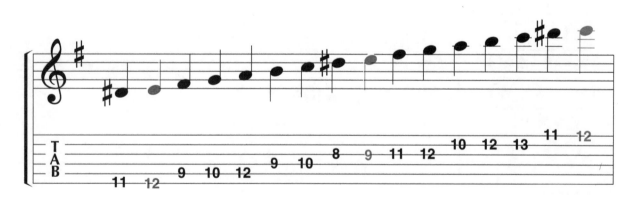

Box Pattern I
12th Position

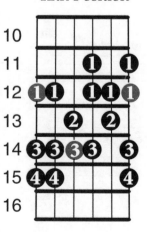

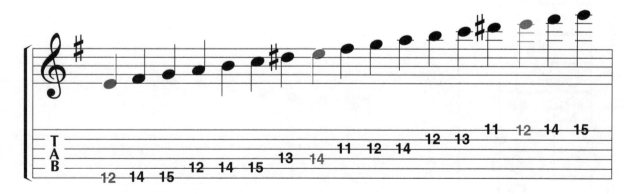

B MINOR SCALES

1st Position

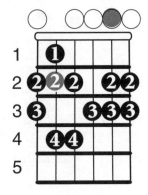

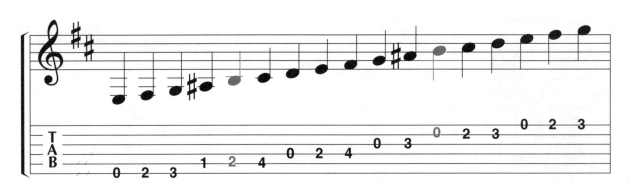

Box Pattern IV
2nd Position

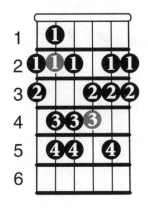

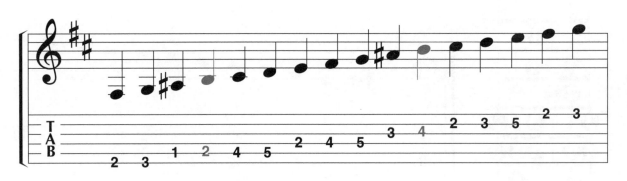

Box Pattern V
4th Position

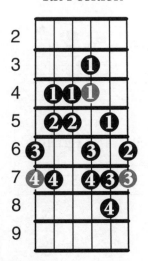

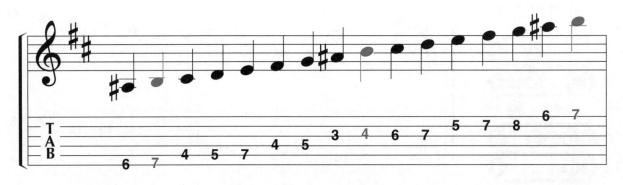

G1032

B Harmonic Minor

B C# D E F# G A# B

Box Pattern I
7th Position

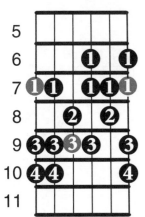

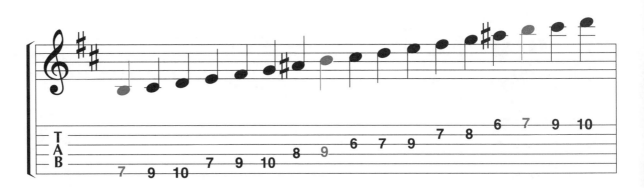

Box Pattern II
9th Position

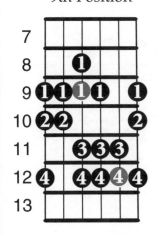

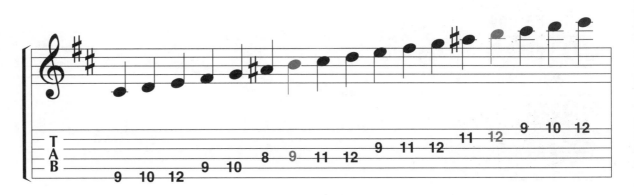

Box Pattern III
12th Position

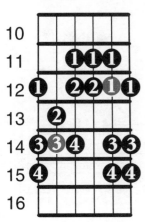

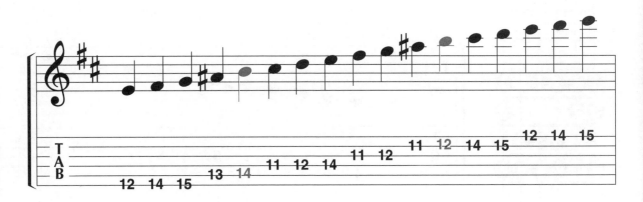

F#/Gb MINOR SCALES

1st Position

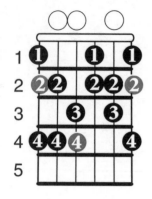

Box Pattern I
2nd Position

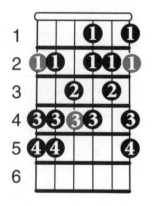
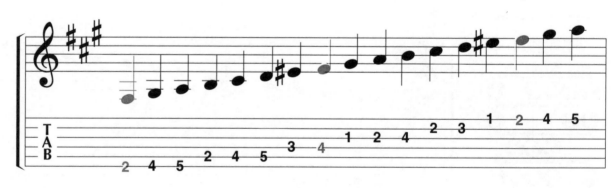

Box Pattern II
4th Position

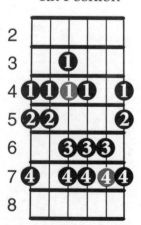

G1032

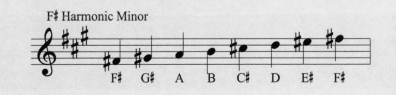

F# Harmonic Minor

F# G# A B C# D E# F#

Box Pattern III
7th Position

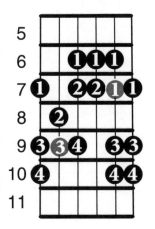

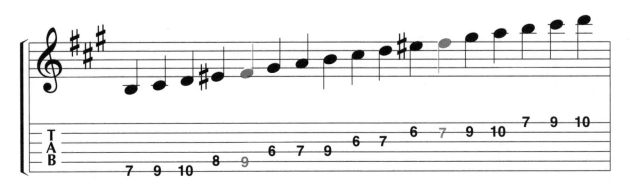

Box Pattern IV
9th Position

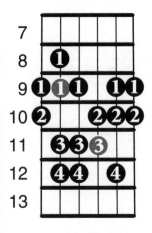

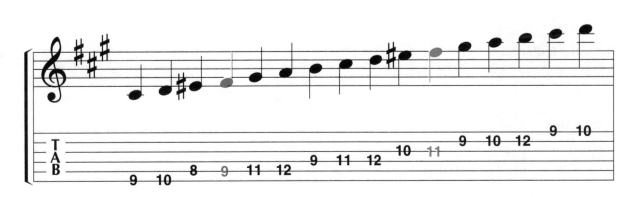

Box Pattern V
11th Position

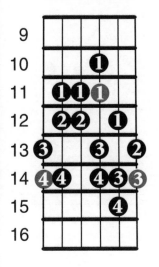

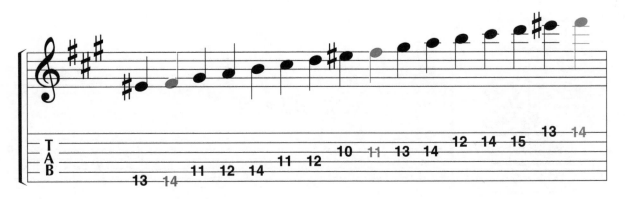

D♭/C♯ MINOR SCALES

1st Position

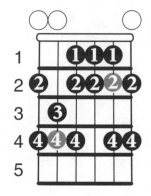

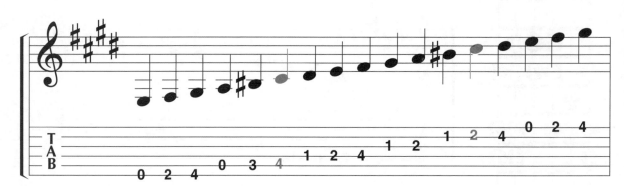

Box Pattern III
2nd Position

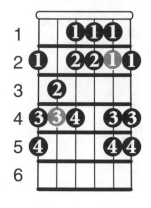

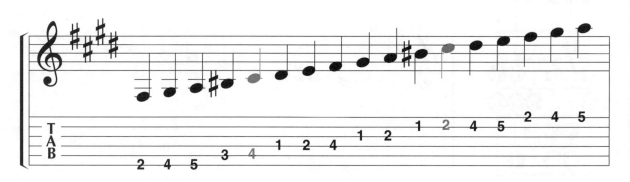

Box Pattern IV
4th Position

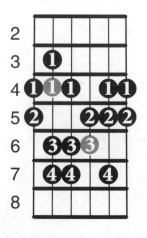

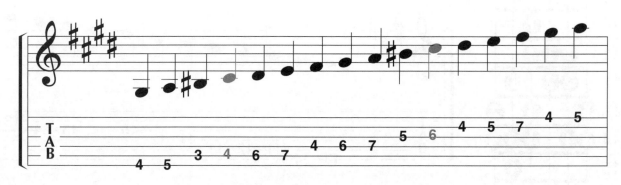

C# Harmonic Minor

C# D# E F# G# A B# C#

Box Pattern V
6th Position

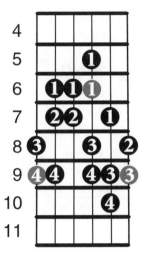

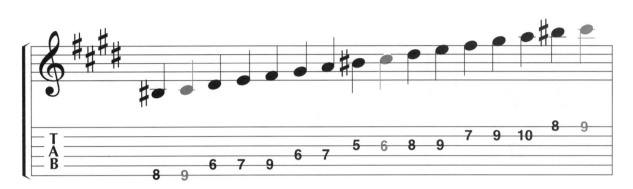

Box Pattern I
9th Position

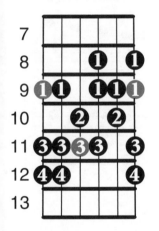

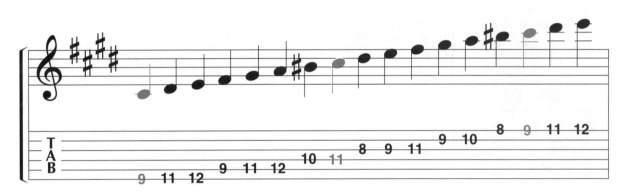

Box Pattern II
11th Position

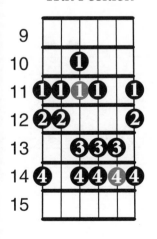

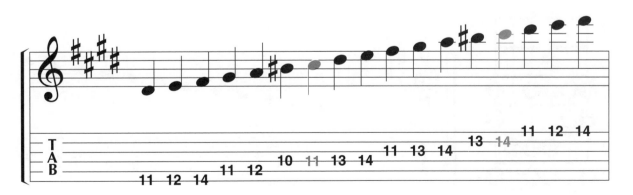

A♭/G♯ MINOR SCALES

1st Position

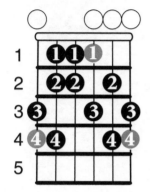
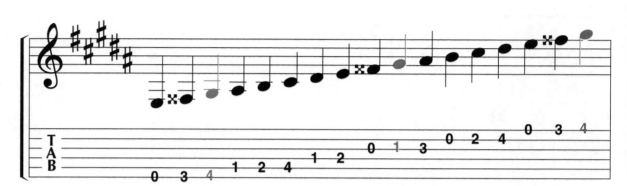

Box Pattern I
4th Position

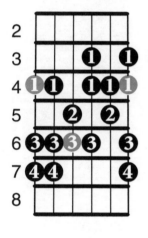
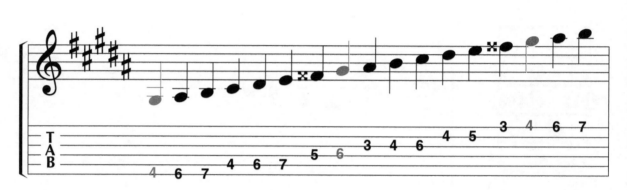

Box Pattern II
6th Position

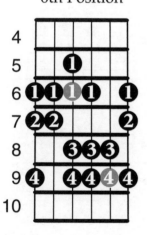

G# Harmonic Minor

G# A# B C# D# E F× G#

Box Pattern III
9th Position

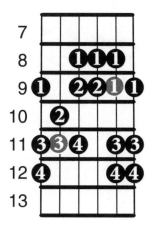

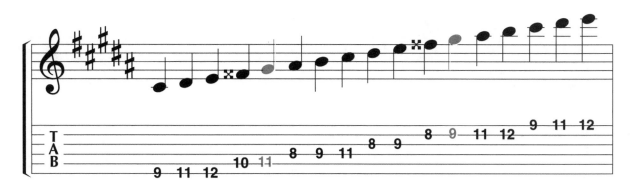

Box Pattern IV
11th Position

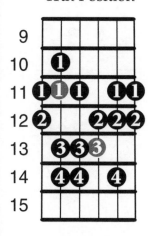

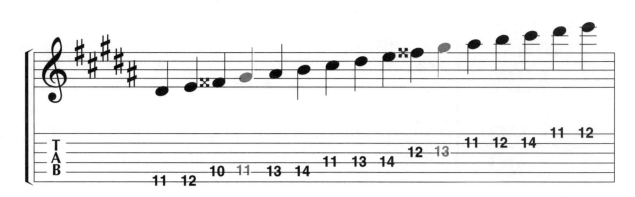

Box Pattern V
13th Position

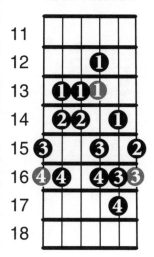

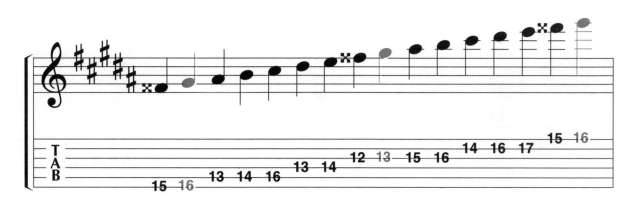

E♭/D♯ MINOR SCALES

1st Position

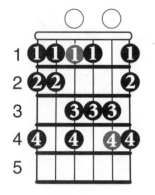
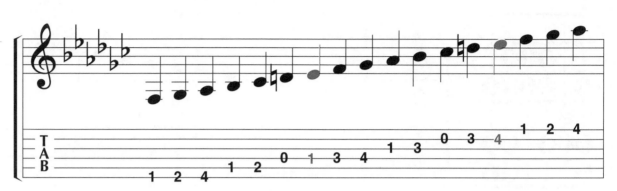

Box Pattern III
4th Position

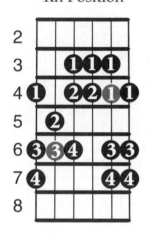
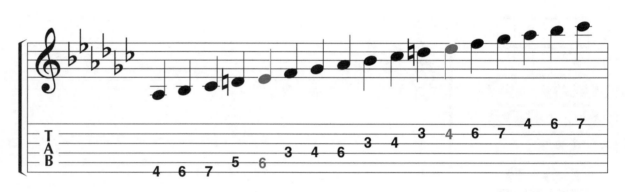

Box Pattern IV
6th Position

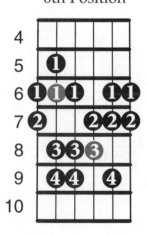
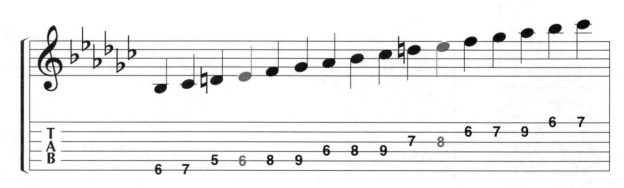

G1032

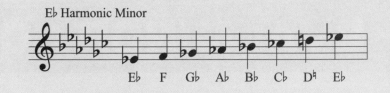

E♭ Harmonic Minor

E♭ F G♭ A♭ B♭ C♭ D♮ E♭

Box Pattern V
8th Position

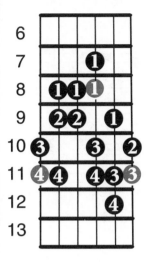

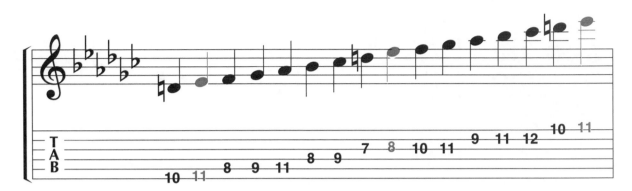

Box Pattern I
11th Position

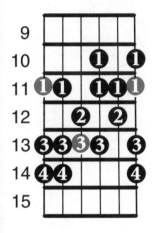

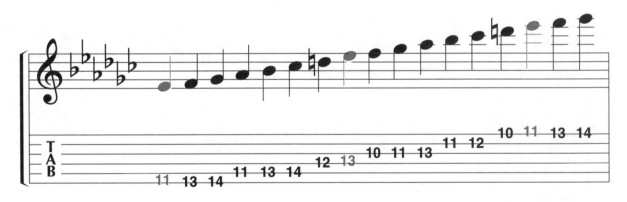

Box Pattern II
13th Position

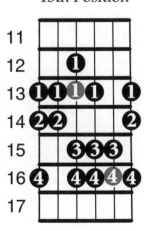

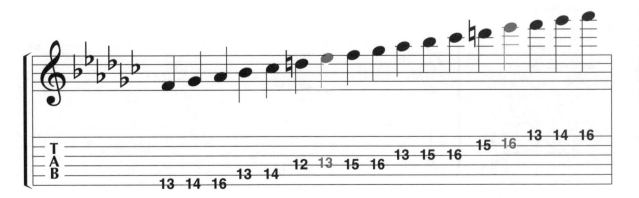

B♭/A♯ MINOR SCALES

1st Position

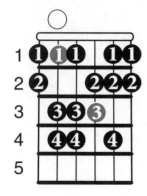

Box Pattern V
3rd Position

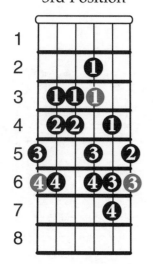

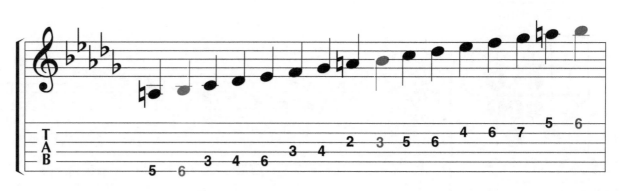

Box Pattern I
6th Position

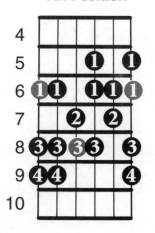

Bb Harmonic Minor

Bb C Db Eb F Gb A♮ Bb

Box Pattern II
8th Position

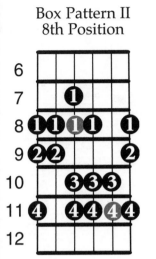

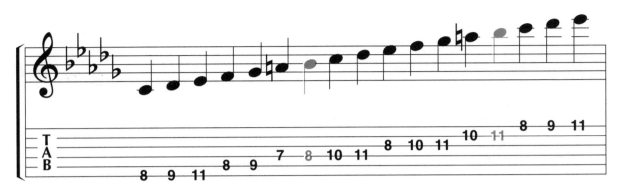

Box Pattern III
11th Position

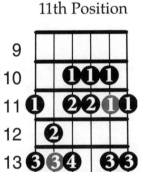

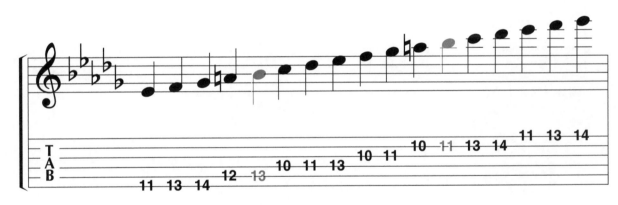

Box Pattern IV
13th Position

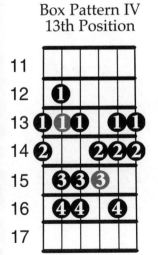

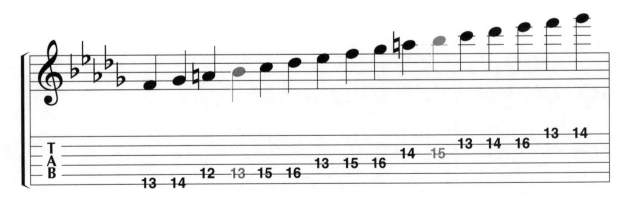

F MINOR SCALES

1st Position

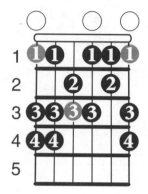
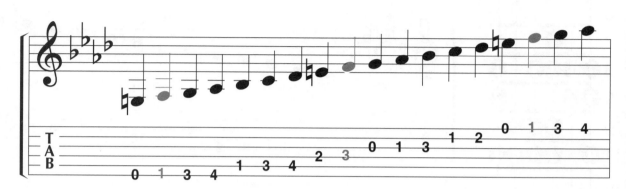

Box Pattern II
3rd Position

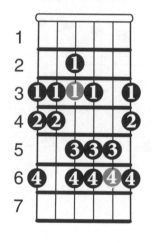

Box Pattern III
6th Position

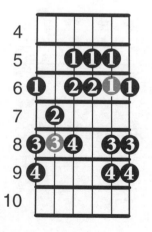

F Harmonic Minor

F   G   Ab   Bb   C   Db   E♮   F

Box Pattern IV
8th Position

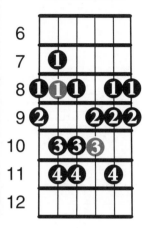

Box Pattern V
10th Position

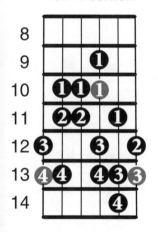

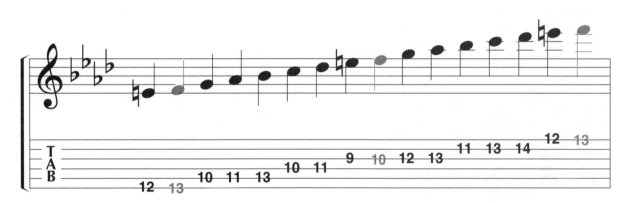

Box Pattern I
13th Position

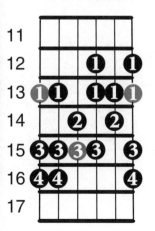

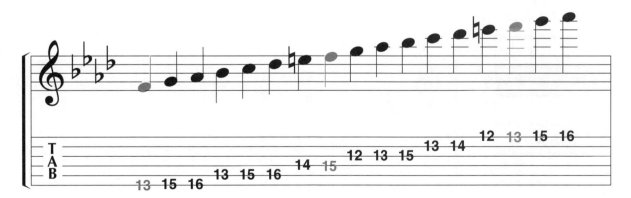

C PENTATONIC SCALES

1st Position

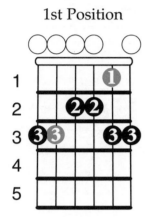

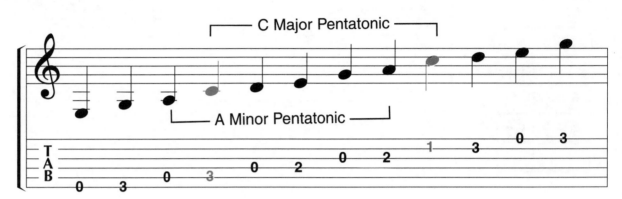

C Major Pentatonic

A Minor Pentatonic

Box Pattern IV
2nd Position

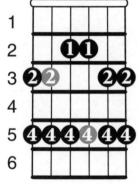

Box Pattern V
5th Position

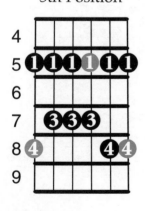

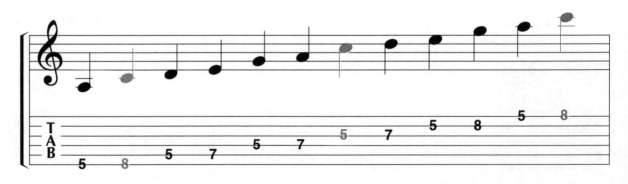

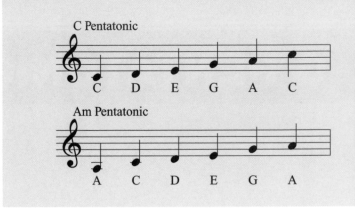

C Pentatonic

C D E G A C

Am Pentatonic

A C D E G A

Box Pattern I
7th Position

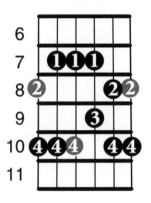

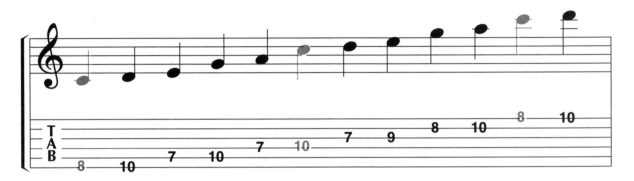

Box Pattern II
9th Position

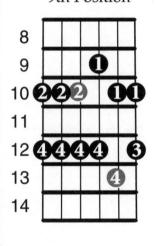

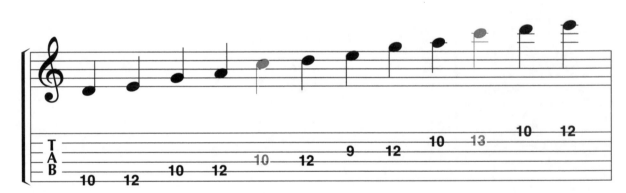

Box Pattern III
12th Position

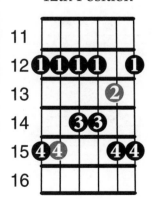

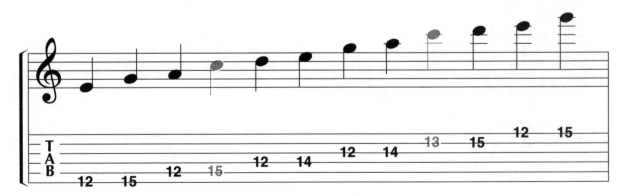

G PENTATONIC SCALES

1st Position

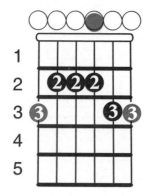

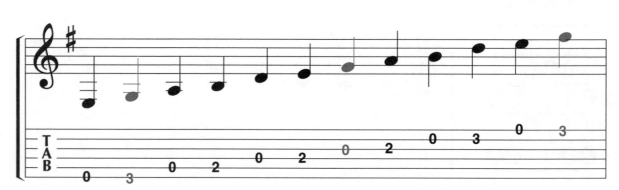

Box Pattern I
2nd Position

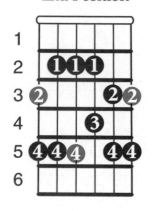

Box Pattern II
4th Position

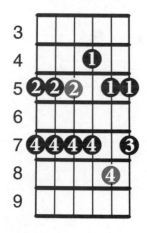

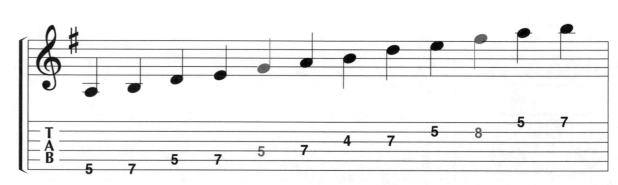

56

G1032

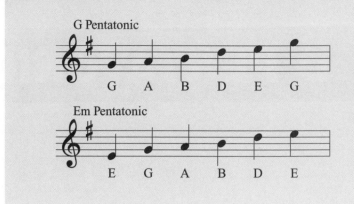

G Pentatonic

G A B D E G

Em Pentatonic

E G A B D E

Box Pattern III
7th Position

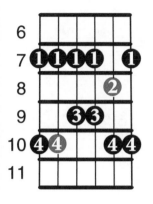

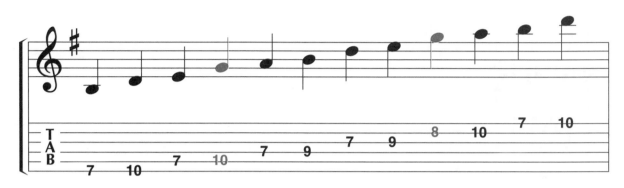

Box Pattern IV
9th Position

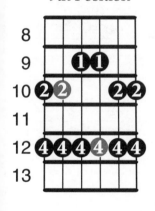

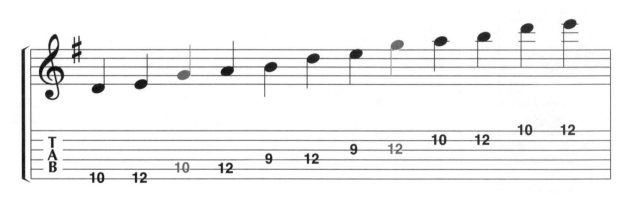

Box Pattern V
12th Position

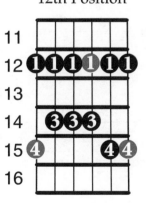

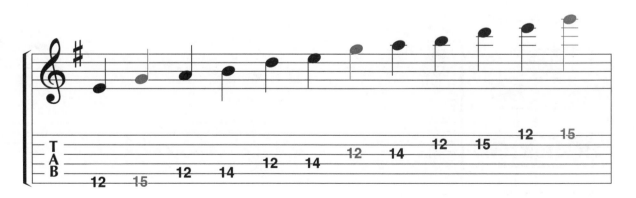

D PENTATONIC SCALES

2nd Position

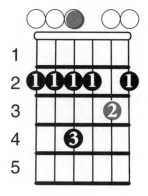

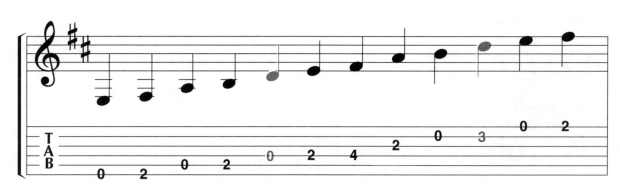

Box Pattern III
2nd Position

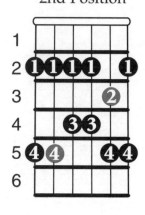

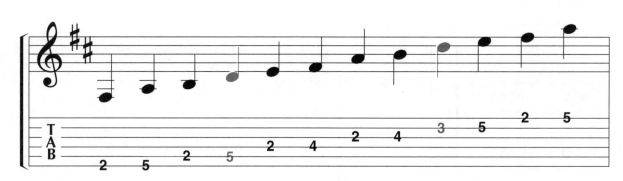

Box Pattern IV
4th Position

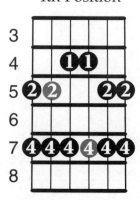

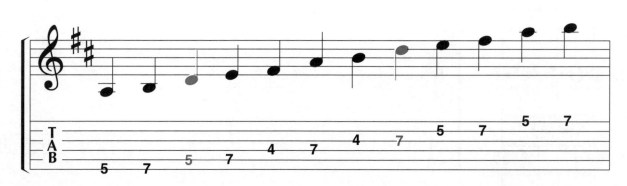

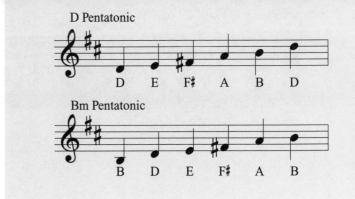

D Pentatonic

D E F# A B D

Bm Pentatonic

B D E F# A B

Box Pattern V
7th Position

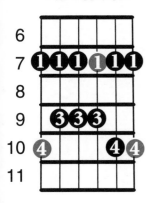

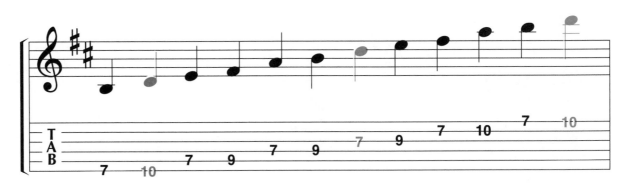

Box Pattern I
9th Position

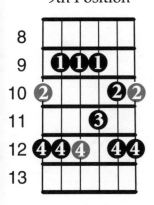

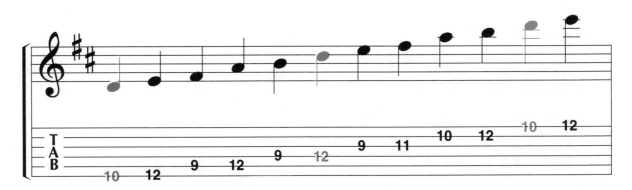

Box Pattern II
11th Position

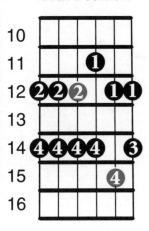

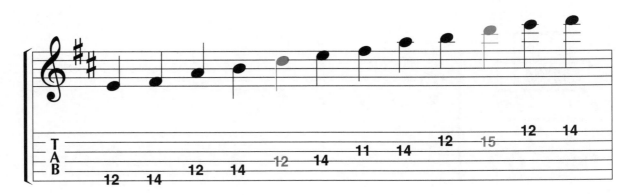

A PENTATONIC SCALES

2nd Position

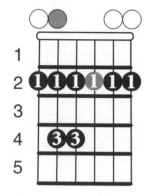

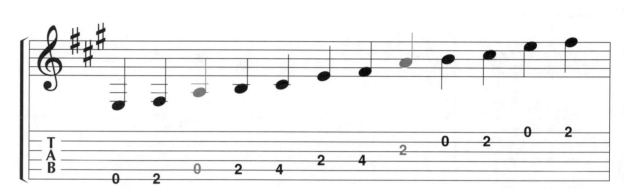

Box Pattern V
2nd Position

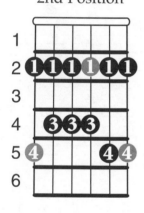

Box Pattern I
4th Position

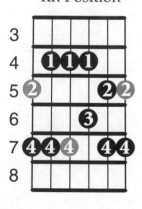

G1032

A Pentatonic

A B C# E F# A

F#m Pentatonic

F# A B C# E F#

Box Pattern II
6th Position

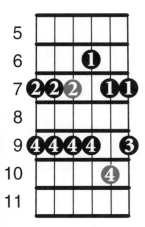

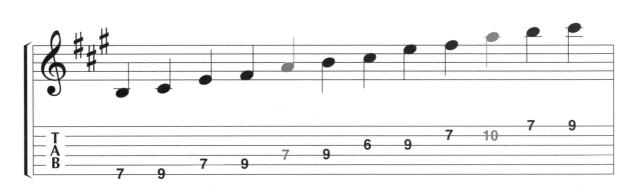

Box Pattern III
9th Position

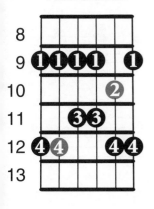

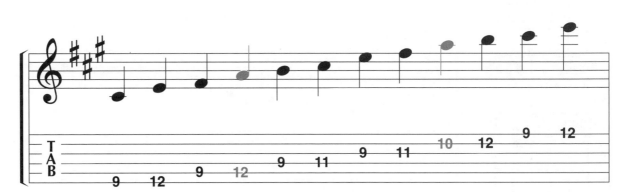

Box Pattern IV
11th Position

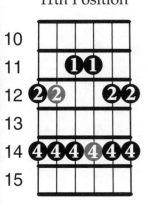

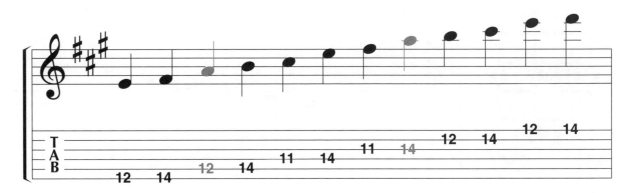

E PENTATONIC SCALES

1st Position

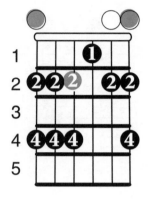
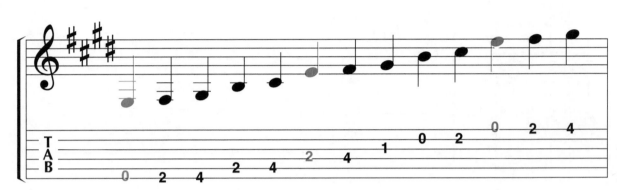

Box Pattern II
1st Position

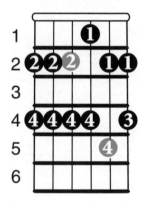
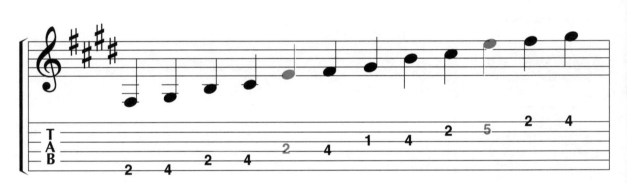

Box Pattern III
4th Position

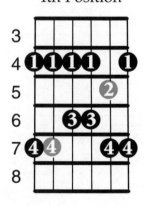

G1032

E Pentatonic

E   F#   G#   B   C#   E

C#m Pentatonic

C#   E   F#   G#   B   C#

Box Pattern IV
6th Position

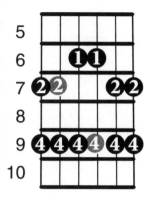

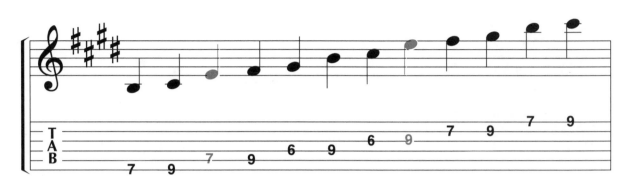

Box Pattern V
9th Position

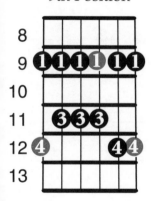

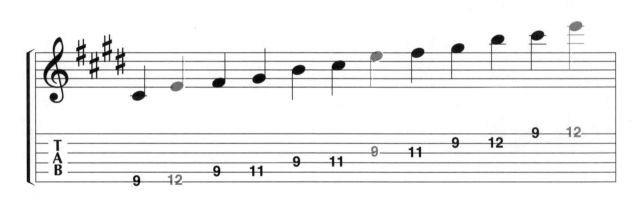

Box Pattern I
11th Position

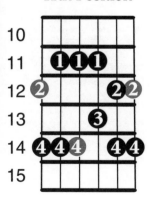

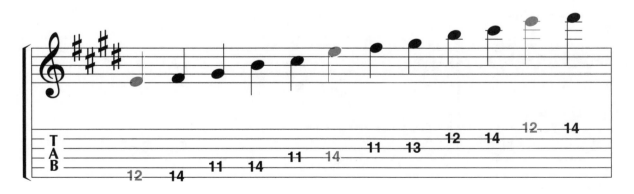

G1032

B PENTATONIC SCALES

1st Position

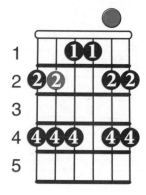

Box Pattern IV
1st Position

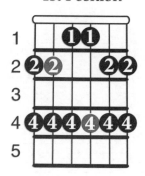
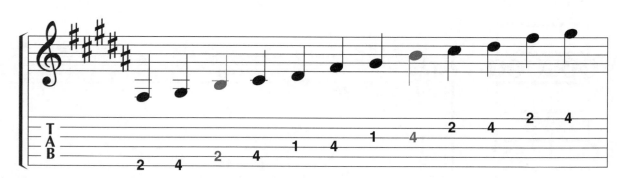

Box Pattern V
4th Position

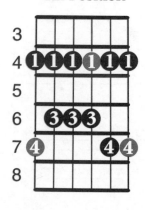
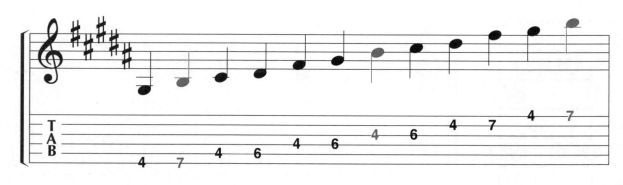

B Pentatonic

B C# D# F# G# B

G#m Pentatonic

G# B C# D# F# G#

Box Pattern I
6th Position

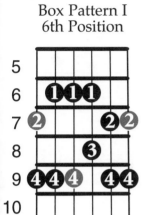

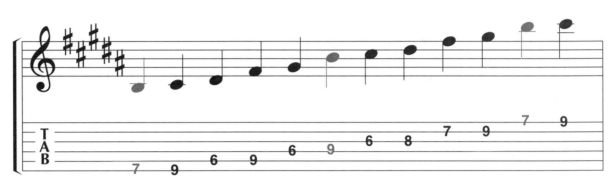

Box Pattern II
8th Position

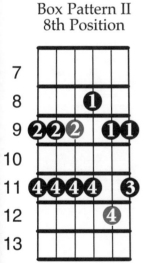

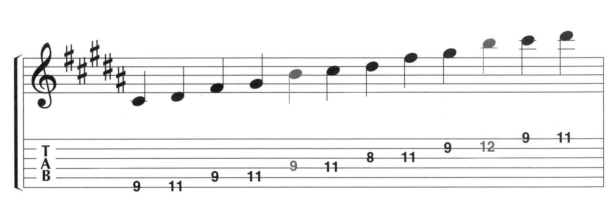

Box Pattern III
11th Position

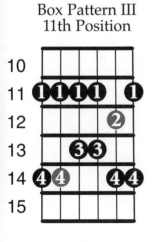

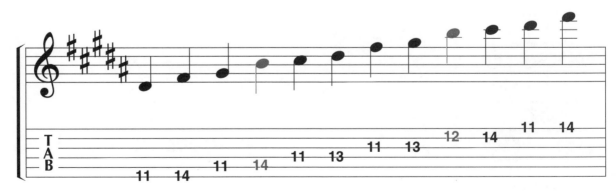

F#/Gb PENTATONIC SCALES

1st Position

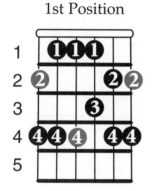

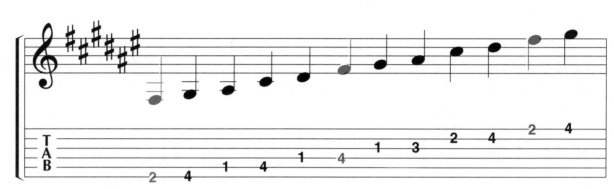

Box Pattern II
3rd Position

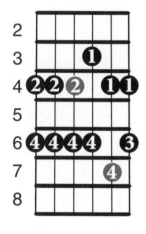

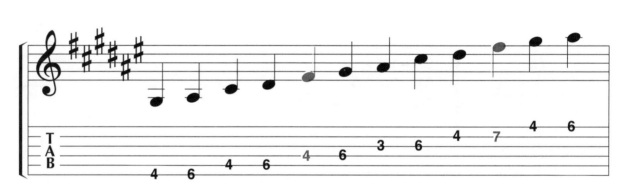

Box Pattern III
6th Position

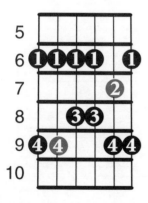

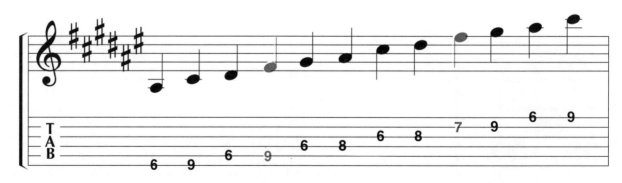

G1032

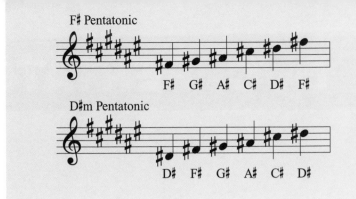

F# Pentatonic

F# G# A# C# D# F#

D#m Pentatonic

D# F# G# A# C# D#

Box Pattern IV
8th Position

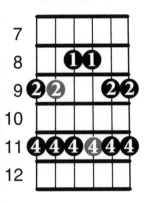

Box Pattern V
11th Position

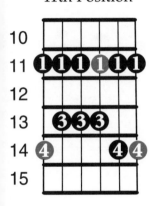

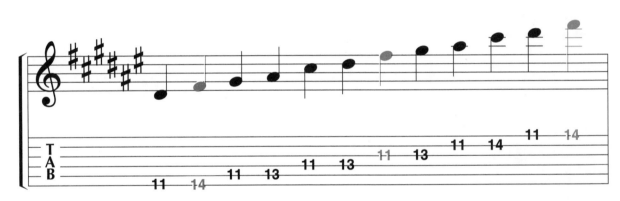

Box Pattern I
13th Position

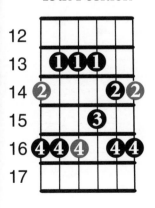

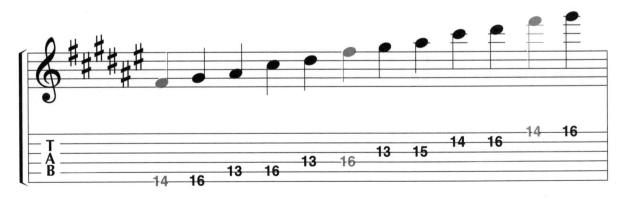

D♭/C♯ PENTATONIC SCALES

1st Position

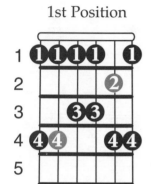
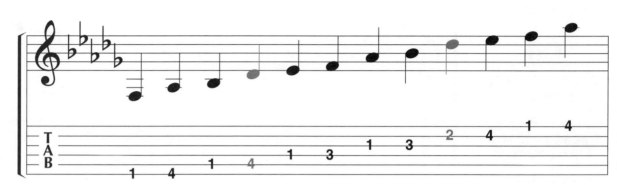

Box Pattern IV
3rd Position

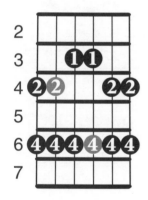
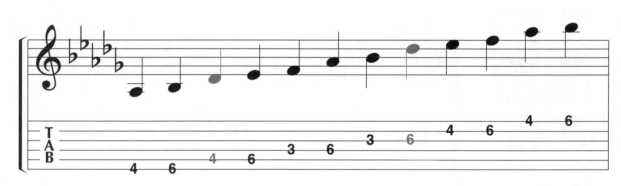

Box Pattern V
6th Position

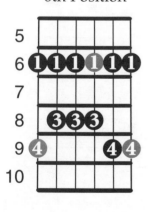
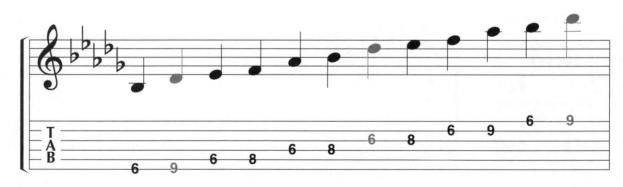

68

G1032

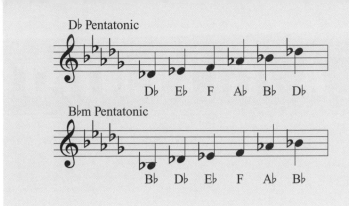

Db Pentatonic

Db Eb F Ab Bb Db

Bbm Pentatonic

Bb Db Eb F Ab Bb

Box Pattern I
8th Position

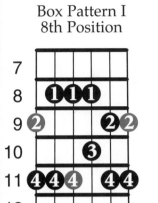

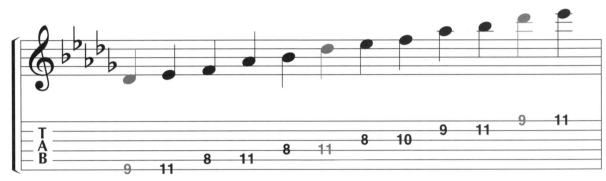

Box Pattern II
10th Position

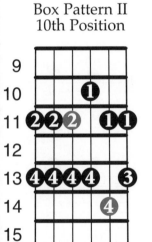

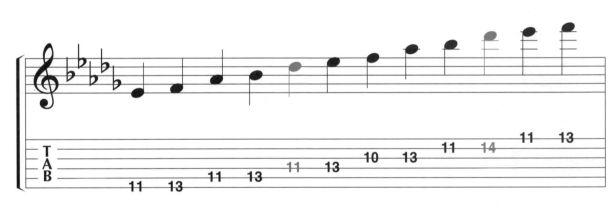

Box Pattern III
13th Position

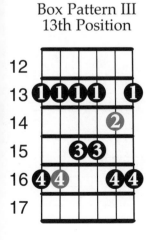

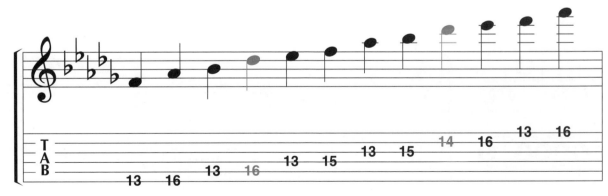

A♭/G# PENTATONIC SCALES

1st Position

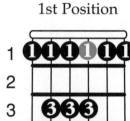

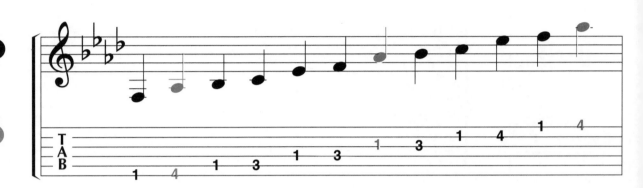

**Box Pattern I
3rd Position**

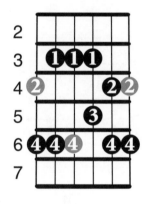

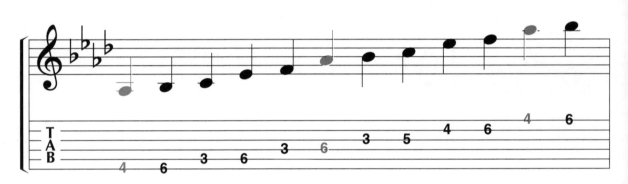

**Box Pattern II
5th Position**

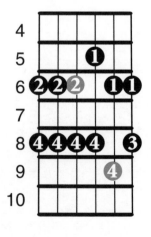

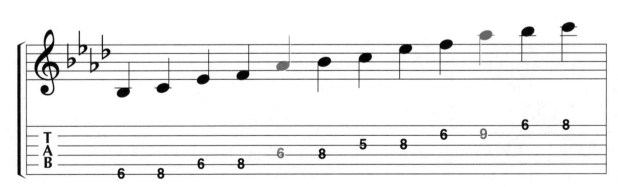

G1032

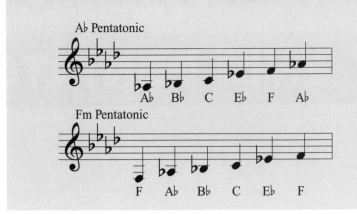

Box Pattern III
8th Position

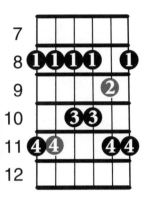

Box Pattern IV
10th Position

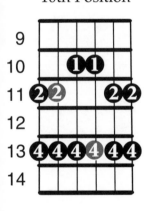

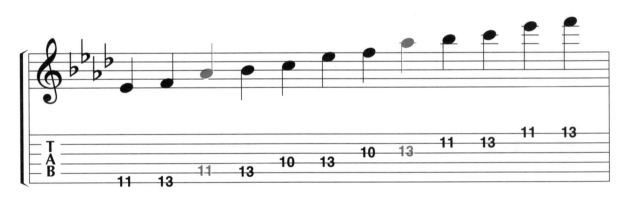

Box Pattern V
13th Position

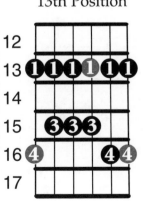

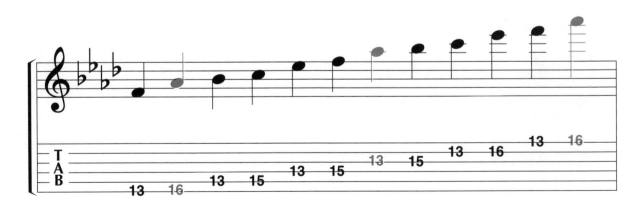

E♭/D♯ PENTATONIC SCALES

1st Position

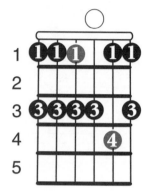
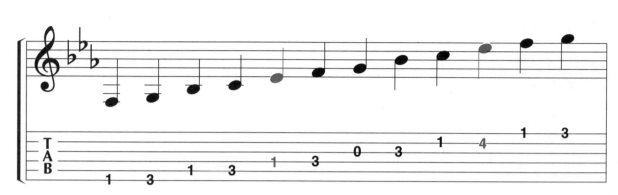

Box Pattern III
3rd Position

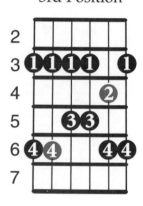

Box Pattern IV
5th Position

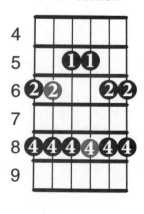
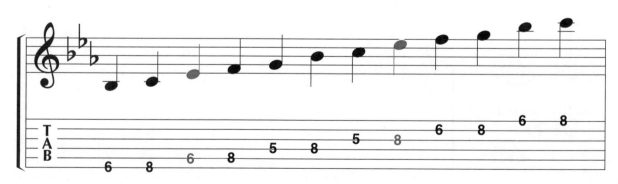

G1032

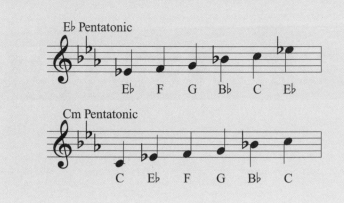

E♭ Pentatonic

E♭   F   G   B♭   C   E♭

Cm Pentatonic

C   E♭   F   G   B♭   C

Box Pattern V
8th Position

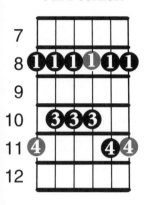

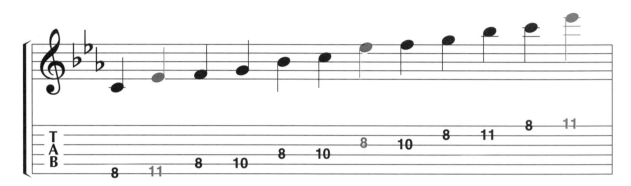

Box Pattern I
10th Position

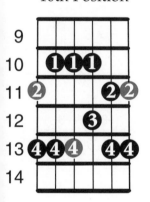

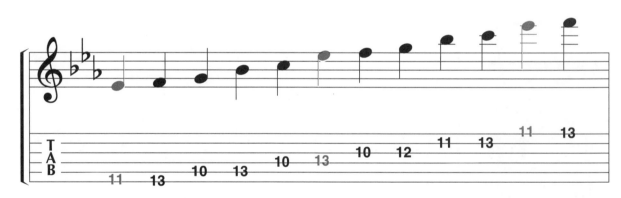

Box Pattern II
12th Position

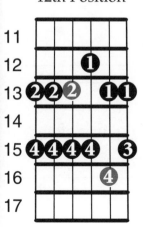

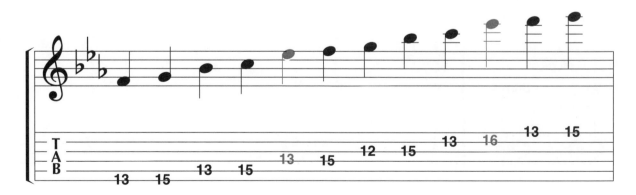

B♭/A♯ PENTATONIC SCALES

1st Position

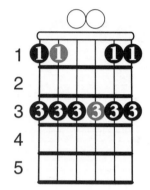

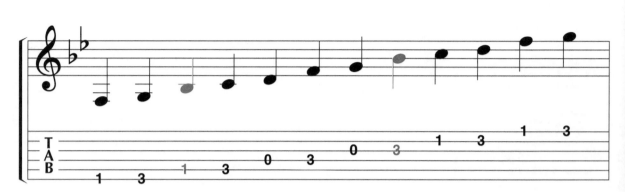

Box Pattern V
3rd Position

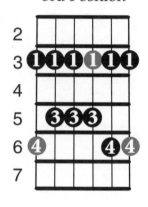

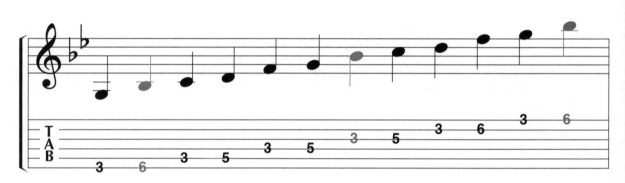

Box Pattern I
5th Position

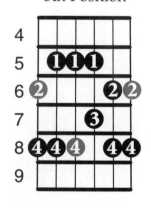

G1032

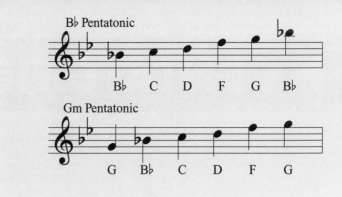

Box Pattern II
7th Position

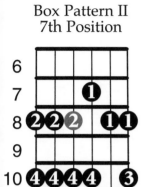

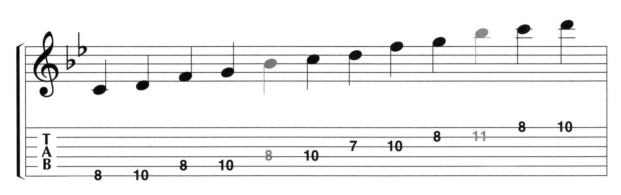

Box Pattern III
10th Position

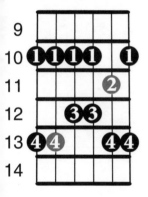

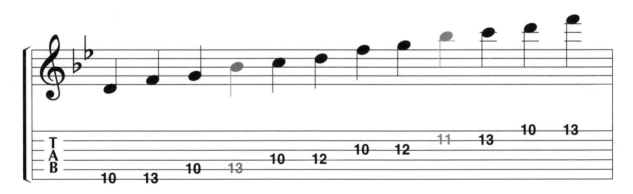

Box Pattern IV
12th Position

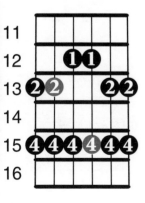

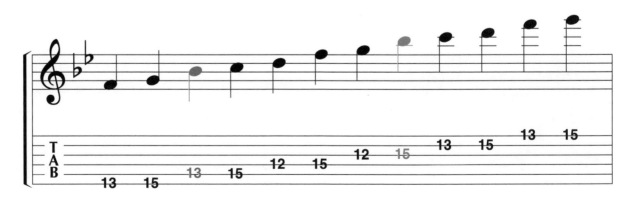

F PENTATONIC SCALES

1st Position

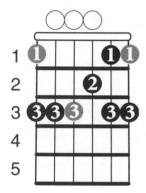

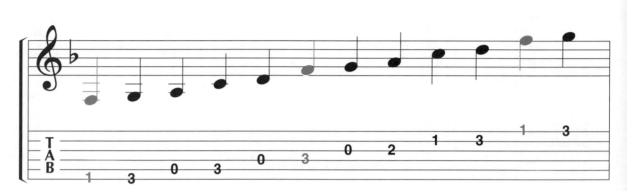

Box Pattern II
2nd Position

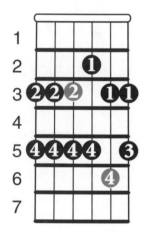

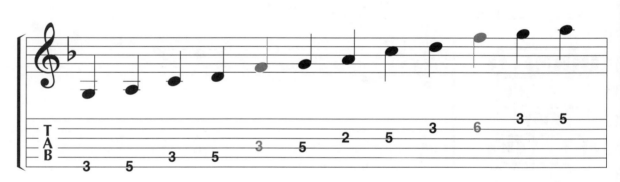

Box Pattern III
5th Position

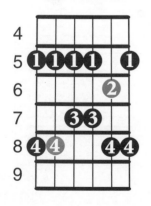

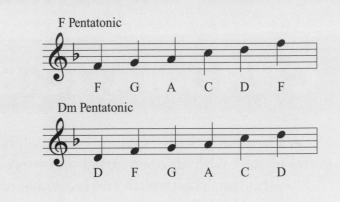

F Pentatonic

F G A C D F

Dm Pentatonic

D F G A C D

Box Pattern IV
7th Position

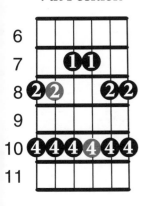

Box Pattern V
10th Position

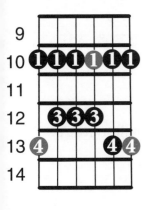

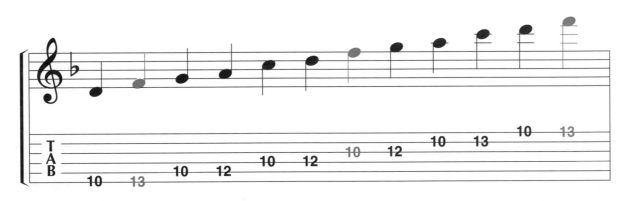

Box Pattern I
12th Position

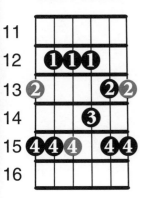

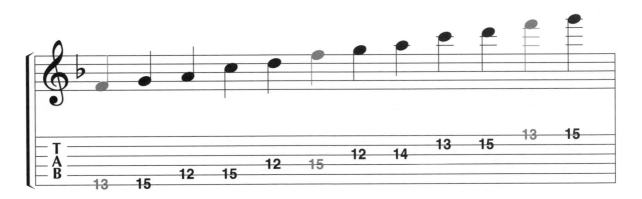

CHROMATIC SCALE

A **Chromatic Scale** is comprised of all half steps. The easiest way to create a chromatic scale is to start with an open string and proceed up the frets numerically until you get to the twelfth fret. The twelfth fret is always one octave higher than the open string. Follow the indicated left-hand fingering.

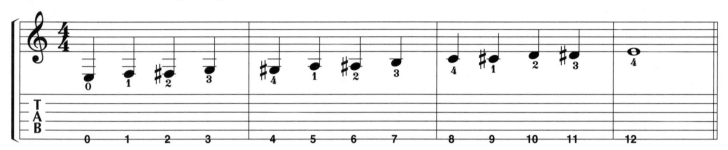

This is a chromatic scale in first position. The finger numbers are identical to the fret numbers.

This is a chromatic scale with no open strings, which means that it is a movable scale pattern.

Use this one octave chromatic scale as an ending. Be sure to start on the root.

Practice the following variations of the C Major Scale, then play them in other keys.

Variation 1

Variation 2

Variation 3

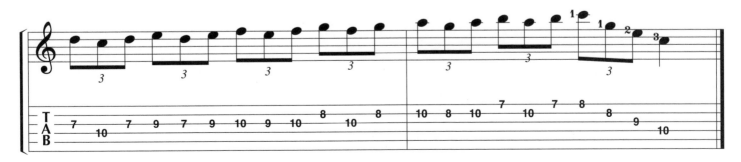

FACT FINDER

TERM	DEFINITION
double flat	(♭♭) Lowers a note by two half steps (two frets).
double sharp	(𝄪) Raises a note by two half steps (two frets).
enharmonic notes	Refers to notes of the same pitch but with different names. The five most common enharmonic notes are: A♯/B♭ C♯/D♭ D♯/E♭ F♯/G♭ G♯/A♭.
flat	(♭) Lowers the pitch of a note by one fret (one half step).
half step	(H) The distance between two notes that are one fret apart.
key	The main note or tonal center of a composition.
legato	Playing in a smooth and connected style.
natural	(♮) Cancels a sharp or flat used earlier.
octave	Two notes that share the same name, and are eight letter names apart.
position playing	Keeping the left-hand fingers over a span of frets. The number indicates the position of the first finger. For example, 2nd Position means the first finger plays all of the notes on the second fret, the second finger plays the third fret, etc.
relative minor	The relative minor scales share the same key signature as their related major scales. The sixth pitch of the major scale denotes the relative minor key. Several examples are: C-Am, G-Em, B♭-Gm.
right-hand fingering	When playing fingerstyle, the right-hand fingers are identified as follows: thumb *p*, index finger *i*, middle finger *m*, and ring finger *a*.
root	The note on which a scale is based (e.g., The root of a C Major scale is C).
sharp	(♯) Raises the pitch of a note by one fret (one half step).
whole step	(W) The distance between two notes that are two frets apart.

G1032